# THE BONE BENEATH THE PULP | DRAWINGS BY WYNDHAM LEWIS

EDITED BY JACKY KLEIN

COURTAULD INSTITUTE OF ART GALLERY

First published 2004 to accompany the exhibition *'The bone beneath the pulp': Drawings by Wyndham Lewis*, 14 October 2004–13 February 2005 at the Courtauld Institute of Art Gallery, London



ISBN 1 903470 26 9

British Library Cataloguing in Publication Data
A catalogue record for this book is available from the British Library.

Produced by Paul Holberton publishing,
37 Snowsfields, London SE1 3SU
www.paul-holberton.net

Designed by Roger Davies
daviesdesign@onetel.com

Printed by Studio Fasoli, Verona, Italy

Front cover: *Self-portrait*, 1911 (cat. 3)
Back cover: *Nude*, 1938 (probably started *c.* 1919) (cat. 42)

All dimensions are in centimetres, height before width. 'M' numbers refer to Walter Michel, *Wyndham Lewis: Paintings and Drawings*, University of California Press, Berkeley and Los Angeles, 1971.

# CONTENTS

# FOREWORD

The Wyndham Lewis Memorial Trust was established in 1980 to promote awareness and understanding of Lewis's work. Since then its trustees have assembled an important collection, including prints, books, archive material and, perhaps of chief interest to Lewis's artistic development, numerous drawings. The significance of the selection shown here lies particularly in its diversity, illustrating not just the radical formal innovations of Vorticism, for which Lewis is perhaps best known, but also his more hesitant beginnings, his promising early engagement with modernism, the portraiture of the 1920s and '30s and the complex work of the 1940s and early '50s, the cumulative significance of which is only gradually being recognised. These drawings chart a sustained career as a visual artist and invite us to reconsider the notion that, Vorticism aside, Lewis should be regarded principally as a literary figure and as an 'outsider' who defined himself entirely through a critical opposition to the cultural developments of his time.

The present exhibition celebrates the long-term loan to the Courtauld Institute of those drawings owned directly by the Wyndham Lewis Memorial Trust. The Trust's long-standing association with the Courtauld was initiated more than ten years ago, when thoughts first turned to securing a future for the collection in which both public access and scholarly enquiry would be actively encouraged. These conditions are amply satisfied at the Courtauld Institute of Art Gallery, where the collection will, moreover, be brought into close and meaningful proximity with that bequeathed to the Institute by Roger Fry on his death in 1934.

The exhibition would not have been possible without the support of the trustees of the Wyndham Lewis Memorial Trust. We are pleased to acknowledge in particular Graham and Vera Lane, whose unflagging enthusiasm has triumphed over various institutional vicissitudes. Cy Fox also deserves our gratitude for his assistance, and for his knowledgeable and charming commentary on the collection which he helped establish, and Prof. Paul Edwards similarly for his authoritative essay. The exhibition would not have its present form without Walter and Harriet Michel's generous personal contribution as well as their long-standing and scholarly commitment to Lewis's work. At the Courtauld special thanks are due to Jacky Klein, the curator of the exhibition, who was very ably assisted by Lucy Askew. Julia Blanks managed the registrarial responsibilities, William Clarke all aspects of conservation, and Peter Carey the photography. Their enthusiasm and commitment allowed the Courtauld to respond at relatively short notice to the opportunity to publish and display this important collection.

Deborah Swallow, *Director, Courtauld Institute of Art*

# PREFACE

Following the death of Wyndham Lewis in 1957, his widow Gladys Anne (Froanna) inherited the copyright in all his paintings, drawings and written work. In 1977 Froanna decided to bequeath these copyrights to her friends Omar Pound and Cy Fox upon their assurance that a charitable trust would be formed to receive the ownership of the copyrights and to administer them with the object of promoting public interest in the visual arts and literature, particularly the work of Wyndham Lewis.

Froanna died on 12 April 1979. The Wyndham Lewis Memorial Trust was established as a registered charity the following year, its founding trustees being Omar Pound, Cy Fox and James Dolman. Since then the Trust has assembled an archive on Wyndham Lewis and his associates, and has acted frequently in support of scholarly publications and exhibitions, including *Wyndham Lewis: Art and War*, held in 1992 at the Imperial War Museum. Another milestone in the revival of interest in Lewis was the publication in 2000 of Paul Edwards's book *Wyndham Lewis: Painter and Writer*. The Trust's principal interest has been locating and, where possible, acquiring paintings and drawings by Lewis in order to place them in the public domain. Notable successes include the acquisition of the important oil from 1937, *Red Portrait*, and the re-emergence, apparently from a collection in India, of a drawing from the *Timon of Athens* series. The loan of its collection to the Courtauld Institute of Art Gallery expresses the Trust's aim to place its material permanently in the public domain and to encourage further research into Lewis's life and career. The Trust has given its full support to the present exhibition of drawings and wishes to thank in particular Dr Ernst Vegelin van Claerbergen, the Courtauld Institute of Art Gallery's Senior Curator, and Jacky Klein, who curated the exhibition with such enthusiasm and expertise.

Following the retirement of Omar Pound in July 2003, the trustees of the Wyndham Lewis Memorial Trust are: Cy Fox, James Dolman, Graham Lane, Paul Edwards, Richard Humphreys, Richard Cork, Brigid Peppin and Walter Michel (honorary trustee).

*The Wyndham Lewis Memorial Trust*

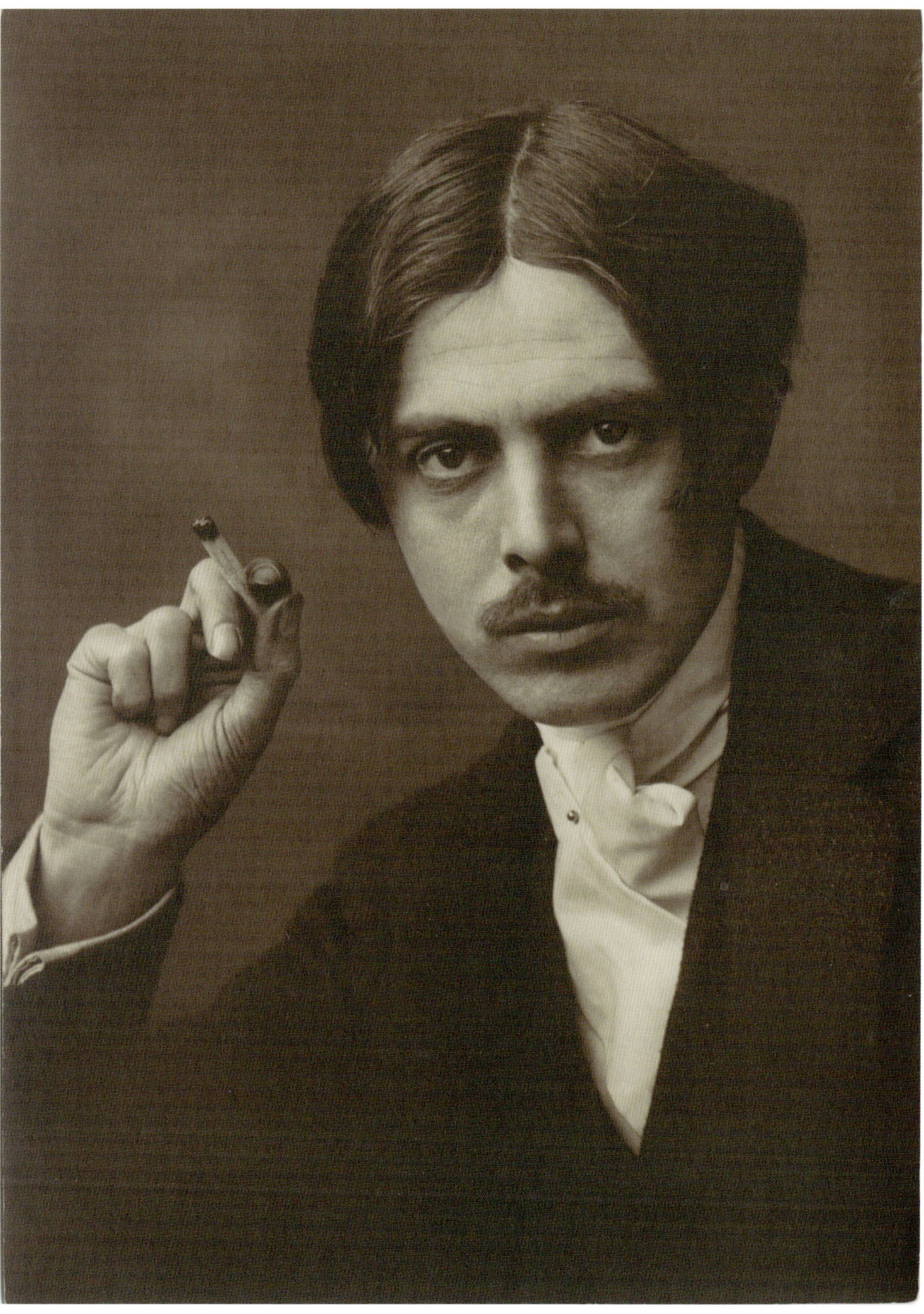

# 'DRAGON IN A CAGE': WYNDHAM LEWIS, 1882–1957

PAUL EDWARDS

In histories of British art in the twentieth century, Wyndham Lewis (fig. 1) occupies a prominent position as the leader of Vorticism, the first real avant-garde movement in England. He is known for his pioneering geometrical abstractions, for the revolutionary typography and dazzling rhetoric of the Vorticist magazine, *Blast*, and for the aggressive, at times paranoid, personality that made him such an unlikely leader of a group. But Lewis's achievement as a painter – also his historical importance – extends far beyond his dominance in the avant-garde of 1913–15, and began before it. Not surprisingly, then, Lewis himself reacted against art historians' concentration on Vorticism, but still acknowledged that the central discipline its rigorous paring-down of visual language had taught him shaped all his later work, giving it structure as bone dictates the shape of flesh. So, in 1950, long after the Vorticist moment, he could still declare, 'I can never feel any respect for a picture that cannot be reduced, at will, to a fine formal abstraction'.[1] In the same year, almost as an emblematic demonstration both of this continuity in his work and, simultaneously, of the distance history and his own imagination had now taken him from that remote moment two world wars away, he took a Vorticist sketch from around 1914, added colour and transformed the structure on the right-hand side into a fantastic, fire-breathing horned monster – *Dragon in a Cage* (cat. 13). The pared-down geometry has been transformed by an exuberant fantasy that it can barely contain.

Fig. 1
Wyndham Lewis, photograph, c. 1912
Division of Rare and Manuscript Collections, Cornell University Library

Many of Lewis's acquaintances testified to his extraordinary improvisatory imagination, how in conversation he could build an extravagant and increasingly fantastic story from a chance observation. He could exercise this capacity with equal virtuosity in both language and paint (or pencil, chalk and pen and ink). Where his imagination operated most excitedly was less in the fantastic subjects he chose to represent (though these tended to become stranger as he grew older) than in the sheer magic of creating images out of the interaction of line, colour and texture on the flat white paper before him, constrained only by the self-imposed limits of visual intelligibility (occasionally not even by that) – a dragon in a cage, indeed. In his visual work it is usually in drawings that his personal language is freest and most inventive. Oil painting demanded a more sustained effort that he was often unable to make, and it is mainly in his paintings of the 1930s that one senses an equivalent pleasure in simply doing unexpected things with the medium. In the present exhibition we can follow this exuberant

1 Wyndham Lewis, *Rude Assignment: A Narrative of my Career up-to-date*, Hutchinson, London, 1950, p. 129.

imagination in a selection of drawings from all periods of Lewis's career, up to the onset of blindness in 1951, when it was debarred from further visual expression and could only find an outlet in writing. For Lewis was not only a painter, he was also a writer, and he is equally important as an innovator in literary modernism – though it is fair to add that he tends to feature less prominently in literary histories than he does in histories of art.

Dualities – of abstraction and representation, or of writing and painting – were fundamental to Lewis. He had a strong sense that only by keeping on the move and refusing to be pinned down with a label could an artist maintain vitality and creativity:

> There is nothing so impressive as the number TWO.
> You must be a duet in everything.
> For the Individual, the single object, and the isolated,
> is, you will admit, an absurdity.
> Why try and give the impression of a consistent
> and indivisible personality?

The article from which this is quoted is headed by the injunction, 'Be Thyself', but Lewis is advocating the development of a multiple personality, one part of which fights for an image of the truth quite different from that which would satisfy the other part of the personality: 'You must catch the clearness and logic in the midst of contradictions: *not* settle down and snooze upon an acquired, easily possessed and mastered, satisfying shape'.[2] It is both the personality of the artist and the version of reality to which the artist adheres that should not be shaped complacently, without a struggle with alternative selves, alternative realities. Shaped by such struggles, Lewis's career is a perfect demonstration of the principle that meaning is generated by difference.

Percy Wyndham Lewis was born in 1882, reputedly on board the yacht of his American father, a wealthy but irresponsible man of leisure and former dragoon officer who served in the Union army during the Civil War.[3] The family moved to the Isle of Wight when Percy was six (he later rejected his given first name and wished to be known simply as Wyndham Lewis) but in 1893 his father ran off with the maid and abandoned the family, remaining an unreliable source of funds while Lewis proceeded through a series of public schools, culminating in two years at Rugby. At the age of sixteen, having neglected academic work, he moved to the Slade School of Art in London, where his drawing won him a scholarship. He was expelled for his lack of diligence two and a half years later. 'All the emphasis was on drawing', Lewis remembered:

> a training was provided of a type so uncraftsmanlike that it surprises me it remained uncriticised. The model of draughtsmanship insisted upon by [Henry] Tonks was cinquecento: but the painting that of an academic, inexact, impressionism ....[4]

2 Wyndham Lewis, 'Vortex No. 1: Art Vortex: Be Thyself', *Blast*, no. 2, July 1915.

3 There are two biographies of Lewis, Jeffery Meyers, *The Enemy: A Biography of Wyndham Lewis*, Routledge & Kegan Paul, London, 1980, and Paul O'Keeffe, *Some Sort of Genius: A Life of Wyndham Lewis*, Jonathan Cape, London, 2000. O'Keeffe's is the more circumstantial and detailed. He throws serious doubt on the possibility that Lewis was actually born on the yacht rather than in the town of Amherst, Nova Scotia.

4 *Rude Assignment*, p. 111.

None of Lewis's student work in oils survives (indeed his earliest surviving oil painting dates from as late as 1914–15), but his early drawings (such as *Alfred de Pass* (?), cat. 1) show why his draughtsmanship, if not his behaviour, satisfied the authorities at the Slade.

For another three years Lewis lived in London, protégé of a circle of intellectuals associated with the British Museum, notably Thomas Sturge Moore and Laurence Binyon. He became known as 'the poet' on the strength of a series of syntactically tortured sonnets he produced at this time. Artistically he was, however, entirely in the shadow of his flamboyant Slade predecessor, Augustus John. Indeed, as late as 1906, he could write to his mother from Normandy (where he was holidaying with John), 'near John I can never paint, since his artistic personality is just too strong'.[5] An odd feature of Lewis's career is that he took so long to emerge as a truly independent writer and painter. He himself dated this emergence to 1908, by which time he had spent four years as a 'student' in Paris (with intervals of travel and study in Holland, Spain and Germany). It may well be that Lewis wanted no trace of his production from these formative years to survive, for none does. His life in Paris is recorded in his first novel, *Tarr*, although the book transposes the self-confident, brash avant-gardist of 1914 back to the Montparnasse of ten years earlier. 'It is dangerous to go to heaven when you are too young. You do not understand it and I did not learn to work in Paris', he later stated.[6] His portrayal of artistic Bohemia in Paris is, accordingly, predominantly satirical: its personae are 'largely ignorant of all but their restless personal lives'.[7] The tortured complexity of his own personal life, particularly his relationship with a German woman to whom he seemed unable to commit himself, but from whom he could not bring himself to part, is also reflected in the novel.

Paris provided him with an education and a European outlook. 'Publishers poured out "libraries" of masterpieces, all the sciences and the arts most daring and up-to-date, priced at a few francs.'[8] Lewis's portrayal of Tarr in the Luxembourg Gardens remembering an occasion 'when he had brought a book to the bench there, his mind tearing at it in advance, almost writing it in its energy' shows the intellectual awakening that now took place. As well as reading the great French and Russian novelists of the nineteenth century, he read Schopenhauer, Nietzsche and Henri Bergson, and attended some of Bergson's lectures at the Collège de France. It was from within these cultural and intellectual traditions that Lewis operated in future, enabling him to be one of the most effective conduits for modernism into England, but also ensuring that he would always seem slightly displaced from the cultural mainstream there. The displacement was exacerbated by his own habitual oppositional stance: the 'other' with whom he maintained a constant struggle was sometimes part of himself, sometimes the whole cultural machinery of London. For, while he was travelling abroad, it seems, he was continually contrasting what he encountered with what he regarded as the cushioned, complacent philistinism of Britain's dominant bourgeoisie (ignoring, as he later admitted, his own position as a privileged spectator who had 'purchased my front-row stall with money derived from that other life I despised').[9]

5 Letter to his mother, undated (dated 1906 by O'Keeffe, p. 72), in *The Letters of Wyndham Lewis*, ed. W.K. Rose, Methuen, London, 1963, p. 39. O'Keeffe reads 'much' instead of 'just'.

6 *Rude Assignment*, p. 113.

7 Wyndham Lewis, *Tarr: The 1918 Version*, ed. Paul O'Keeffe, Black Sparrow Press, Santa Barbara, 1990, p. 21.

8 *Rude Assignment*, p. 113.

9 *Ibid.*, p. 117.

Through his accounts of some of these travels, and stories derived from them filled with comic paradox and brilliant observation, Lewis began to be known in England after returning in 1908. The subject of these pieces was the 'primitive' life of the peasants and fishermen of Brittany and coastal Spain. Here, apparently, was 'authentic' natural life of the kind that early modernists valued as an alternative to the instrumental and functional rationalism of modernity. 'The body knows better than the mind' is a doctrine that could be deduced from the philosophers Lewis had been reading, particularly Bergson. 'Civilisation', notably such English institutions as sport, cordons off the body and its energies into areas of make-believe and play, so life becomes impoverished and unreal. Such was the argument of Lewis's 1910 essay, 'Our Wild Body'.[10] In visual form the 'wild bodies' came alive in drawings like *Two Muscular Figures* (cat. 9), their proportions shaped by their own physical sense of muscle-bound inflation.

But these bodies (and others in Lewis's work – even, perhaps, Nijinski's, cat. 11 and 12) are also faintly ridiculous. Drawing is physical, dependent on the executant's musculature, but it can also be the most intellectual of visual arts, and the drawn line is the purest symbol of an idea. Lewis's imaginative identification with his wild bodies came to be inflected with a sardonic detachment, as he deconstructed, both in painting and in writing, the simplicities of naïve primitivism. The 'authentic' impulses of the body might simply be no more than automatic responses to delusional motives, or habits brought into being by larger social structures, not unmediated acts emerging from the body's intuitive knowledge. Lewis worked through the implications of this possibility in an essay, 'Inferior Religions', published later with revised versions of his early writings.[11] Confronted with the pathos of the primitive *Figure holding a Flower* (cat. 7), we do not know whether to sympathise or laugh – a discomforting effect that Lewis, poised between these reactions himself, intends us to ponder.

In the art world of London, Lewis now became uneasily associated both with the Camden Town Group and with Roger Fry, though his work was now showing the influence of Cubism, as can be seen from the 1911 *Self-portrait* (cat. 3). Such work hardly fitted the ethos of Camden Town, and he was admitted as a member largely because of his friendship with Spencer Gore, against the wishes of Walter Sickert. Because of the strong formal qualities of his painting he was more likely to be appreciated by Fry, but personally he was highly antithetical to Bloomsbury (Duncan Grant wrote that 'my gorge simply rises when ever I see him')[12] It was in 1912, nearly at the age of 30, that Lewis became a major force in English art and began showing the energy and inventiveness that by 1914 would make him the recognised leader of the avant-garde. With Spencer Gore and other artists he supplied decorations for Frida Strindberg's nightclub, 'The Cave of the Golden Calf'. His nine-foot-square painting, *Kermesse*, depicting primitive figures in a wild dance, hung above the door (only a small ink and watercolour sketch now survives, fig. 2). At the Second Post-Impressionist Exhibition he exhibited two paintings (both known only from photographs) and eight drawings, one of which, *A Masque of Timon* (cat. 6), shows a new influence from Futurism.

10 'Our Wild Body', *The New Age*, 5 May 1910, in Wyndham Lewis, *The Complete Wild Body*, ed. Bernard Lafourcade, Black Sparrow Press, Santa Barbara, 1982, pp. 251–56.

11 Wyndham Lewis, *The Wild Body: 'A Soldier of Humour' and Other Stories* (1927), Penguin, London, 2004; also in *The Complete Wild Body*, which also prints earlier versions of the texts, including 'Inferior Religions', which dates from 1914.

12 Duncan Grant, letter to Lytton Strachey, 18 February 1908, quoted in O'Keeffe, *Some Kind of Genius*, p. 80.

13 'Round Robin', October 1913, in *Letters*, ed. Rose, p. 4.

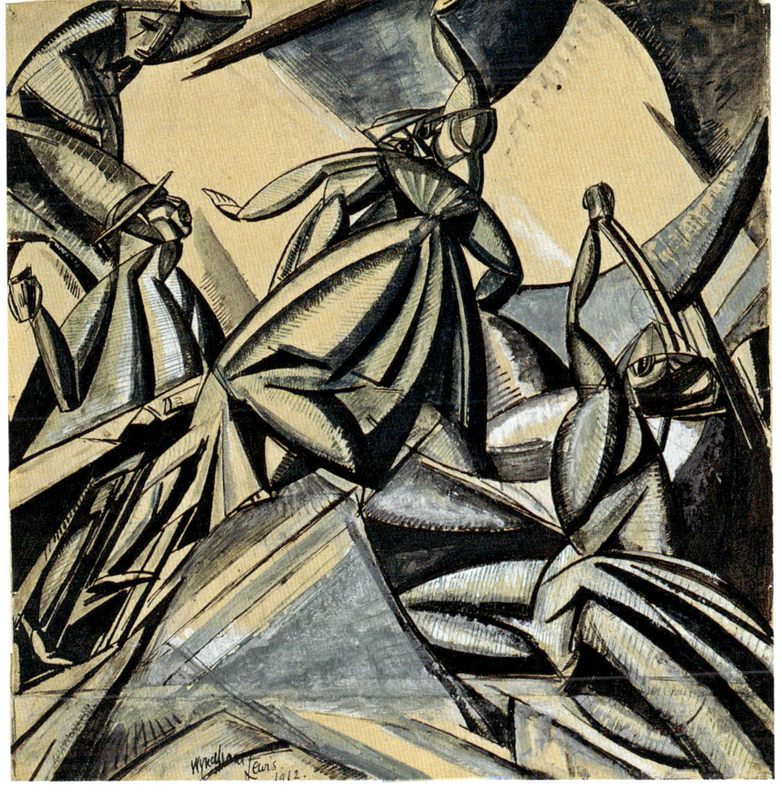

Fig. 2
*Study for Kermesse*, 1912, pen and ink, pencil, gouache and watercolour on paper, 30.5 × 30.6 [M72] Yale Center for British Art, New Haven (Paul Mellon Fund and gift of Neil F. and Ivan E. Phillips in memory of their mother, Mrs Rosalie Phillips)

Lewis joined Roger Fry's Omega Workshops on its founding in spring 1913, but walked out in October, convinced that Fry had misappropriated for the Omega a valuable commission (part of which was intended for Lewis personally) to decorate a room at the Ideal Home Exhibition. Despite Fry's protestations of innocence, Lewis persuaded fellow artists Edward Wadsworth, Frederick Etchells and Cuthbert Hamilton to join his defection; all would be members of the Vorticist group early the following year. Lewis's parting blast was a letter of denunciation sent to prominent Omega patrons and the press:

> The Idol is still Prettiness, with its mid-Victorian languish of the neck, and its skin is 'greenery-yallery', despite the Post-What-Not fashionableness of its draperies. This family party of strayed and Dissenting Aesthetes, however, were compelled to call in as much modern talent as they could find, to do the rough and masculine work without which they knew their efforts would not rise above the level of a pleasant tea-party, or command more attention.[13]

Lewis had learned the aggressive masculinism of this rhetoric from F.T. Marinetti's Futurist manifesto, with its professed 'scorn for women'.

It seemed that he had elected to become a Futurist, for in November he was co-host with C.R.W. Nevinson of a dinner given for Marinetti. Also with Nevinson, he planned the launch of a magazine in support of the new avant-garde effort, to be called, at Nevinson's suggestion, *Blast*. In January 1914, Kate Lechmere, a painter friend, proposed opening a kind of *atelier*, and in March the Rebel Art Centre opened under Lewis's direction on premises rented by Lechmere. It was hung with draperies even more fashionable than those of the Omega, but not many of its advertised activities took place. Lewis was both too incompetent and too jealous of his privileges to make a success of the venture. But the 'unauthorised' use of its address for a manifesto, 'Vital English Art', issued by Marinetti and Nevinson in June 1914, provided a pretext for yet another split. Feeling themselves too closely identified with – and too much in the shadow of – Futurism, the Rebel Art Centre group publicly rebuked Nevinson and Marinetti, and in July, with the publication of the first issue of *Blast*, launched the English avant-garde movement, Vorticism, complete with its own manifesto and illustrations of its particular style of geometric abstraction. The signatories to the manifesto were Richard Aldington, Malcolm Arbuthnot, Lawrence Atkinson, Jessica Dismorr, Henri Gaudier-Brzeska, Cuthbert Hamilton, Ezra Pound, William Roberts, Helen Saunders, Edward Wadsworth and Lewis himself. Jacob Epstein and David Bomberg, though to some extent associated with the group, declined to join.

The sources of Vorticist abstraction, or at least of Lewis's, were various – the visual styles and aesthetics of Cubism, Expressionism (Kandinsky's in particular) and Futurism; the aesthetic ideas of Roger Fry and Clive Bell; Wilhelm Worringer's idea of abstraction, mediated through the anti-Romantic poet-philosopher T.E. Hulme; the exposition of the aesthetics of oriental art found in Laurence Binyon's *The Flight of the Dragon*.[14] Lewis's own position as articulated in *Blast* and manifested in his own paintings was created by an interlocking set of differences from these 'sources'.

Lewis's new ally, the American poet Ezra Pound, wanted Vorticism to be a movement of writers as much as of painters. Agreeing with him, Lewis nevertheless thought that the delicate *japonaiserie* of Pound's imagism, his antiquarian pastiches and epigrams, hardly qualified as an equivalent to Vorticist painting. His own Vorticist play, *Enemy of the Stars*, printed in the first issue of *Blast*, was intended to supply what was lacking. The two main characters were representations of one of Lewis's 'duets', another pair of muscular figures:

14 Laurence Binyon, *The Flight of the Dragon: An Essay on the Theory and Practice of Art in China and Japan*, John Murray, London, 1911. Chapter 4, 'The Emergence of Vorticism', of Paul Edwards, *Wyndham Lewis: Painter and Writer*, Yale University Press, London and New Haven, 2000, attempts to tease out the various 'sources' of Vorticism in detail.

CHARACTERS.

| TWO HEATHEN CLOWNS, | GRAVE BOOTH ANIMALS<br>CYNICAL ATHLETES. |
|---|---|

DRESS. ENORMOUS YOUNGSTERS, BURSTING EVERY-WHERE THROUGH HEAVY TIGHT CLOTHES, LABOURED IN BY DULL EXPLOSIVE MUSCLES, full of fiery dust and sinewy energetic air, not sap. BLACK CLOTH CUT SOMEWHERE, NOWADAYS, ON THE UPPER BALTIC.

VERY WELL ACTED BY YOU AND ME.[15]

It is a violent, Expressionist *agon*, set in a Vorticist space, fringed by a canal, 'the night pouring into it like blood from a butcher's pail'. There, two versions of the self fight and destroy each other.[16] No-one else in England was writing like this.

A month after the publication of *Blast*, the First World War broke out. There was a Vorticist exhibition in 1915, and another in New York in 1917, comprising work that the enterprising Ezra Pound had persuaded the American collector John Quinn to buy, but the movement was not to survive the war. Lewis set about ordering his visual and literary oeuvre (making Pound his executor) ready for his expected departure for the Front. He was by now the father of two children, but appears to have had a rather on–off relationship with their mother, Olive Johnson, and he did not allow it to cramp his style. In 1915 he was infected with gonorrhoea, which neglect turned to septicaemia, and in the enforced leisure he revised the novel he had drafted in 1911, *Tarr*. With Pound's help it was placed in *The Egoist*, to be serialised after James Joyce's *A Portrait of the Artist as a Young Man*. After a second 'War Number' of *Blast* and the Vorticist exhibition, Lewis enlisted in March 1916 and began training that would culminate in his being sent as a lieutenant in the Royal Garrison Artillery to France in time to participate in the battle of Messines in June 1917. With an interval of trench fever, he was to remain with the artillery until virtually the end of the Third Battle of Ypres ('Passchendaele'), from which he returned to London in November to visit his mother when she was hospitalised with flu. He returned as a War Artist in January 1918, commissioned by the Canadian scheme for a painting of a heavy gun in action and, later, by the British scheme for a similar subject. *A Battery shelled* was completed in 1919 and is now in the Imperial War Museum.

The war had a profound effect on Lewis personally, as it did on the cultural climate of the post-war period. Kate Lechmere believed he had suffered emotional damage, and found him soured and embittered.[17] But what she took for a loss of spontaneity may simply have been a more deliberate determination. His immediate response to peace was to attempt to renew the avant-garde effort in painting and extend it into 'our common life' of design, architecture and town-planning. A polemical pamphlet, *The Caliph's Design*, outlined his case but also

15 Wyndham Lewis, *Enemy of the Stars*, *Blast*, no. 1, July 1914, p. 55.

16 *Ibid.*, p. 62.

17 Kate Lechmere's remarks as reported in J.B. Harmer, *Victory in Limbo: Imagism 1908–1917*, Secker & Warburg, London, 1975, p. 180.

provided a critique of the incipient 'return to order' and classicism in Paris and of the timid aestheticism of Bloomsbury.[18] It was a modernism for English conditions that Lewis wished to establish, 'perfectly interpenetrated with Western European culture, and yet using that culture independently with a freedom considered barbarous by the French'.[19] Lewis was persuaded to become the leader of 'Group X', who held a show in 1920, but the centre of power in London art politics was now with Fry and Bloomsbury, and the group failed to thrive. Lewis was now known as much for his writing as for his painting, and was as closely associated with the literary avant-garde of Pound, T.S. Eliot (whose first publication in England was in *Blast*, no. 2) and James Joyce (fig. 3) as he was with painters. He went on holiday to France with Eliot, and in Paris spent the days looking at Chinese art and the evenings dining and drinking with Joyce. His parental responsibilities back home had increased, in the form of two children by Iris Barry, born in 1919 and 1920. Barry was the subject of many of Lewis's drawings from 1919 to 1921, when they seem to have parted, and the model for his painting *Praxitella* of 1921 (Leeds City Art Gallery), a good example of the 'barbarism' of Lewis's modernism at this time.

England was not hospitable to any form of modernism, however. Ezra Pound left in disgust, and Lewis had to decide whether to follow him to Paris. Léonce Rosenberg offered him a show of his more advanced work (of which *Women*, cat. 23, is a good example) at l'Effort Moderne gallery, but Lewis failed to take advantage of the offer; his one-man show of 'Tyros and Portraits' at the Leicester Galleries in 1921 had not pleased the critics, and by 1923–24 painting had become secondary to writing in his career – or at least in the public presentation of it. For he still produced work that showed the prominence he might have achieved had there been a place for advanced work in England (for example, *Three Sisters*, cat. 25). For those who value him primarily as a painter, the priority he now gave to writing is regrettable, but at this moment Lewis had things to say that he could only express through writing. He retreated to the British Museum Reading Room and to his study, emerging again in public in 1926 as the author of *The Art of Being Ruled*, a political treatise, and in 1927 as editor and chief writer of a new magazine, *The Enemy*. Its contents consisted chiefly of a scathing critique primarily of the literary avant-garde for its failure to achieve anything more than superficial novelty. What had not been achieved, he argued, was a thorough, radical revaluation of the ideological bases of post-war culture in a genuinely revolutionary art. Two of the most prominent targets were Ezra Pound and James Joyce, Lewis's need to establish difference having led him to a betrayal of the friendship of his associates. Lewis's life was by now strewn with examples of unfeeling selfishness, not least the failure of care for the children he had fathered and, as his own father had him, virtually abandoned.

Lewis's critique of the avant-garde was part of a much larger project. Vorticism had aimed at adjusting public consciousness to the culture of modernity, but war had meant that, in all areas of public culture, this adjustment had been distorted and unsuccessful. Lewis, with an ambition that on the face of it would seem fatally disproportionate to his skills as a novelist and a visual artist,

18 Wyndham Lewis, *The Caliph's Design: Architects! Where is your Vortex?* (1919), ed. Paul Edwards, Black Sparrow Press, Santa Barbara, 1986.

19 'Foreword', *Group X*, Mansard Gallery, London, 1920, in *Wyndham Lewis on Art: Collected Writings 1913–1956*, ed. Walter Michel and C.J. Fox, Thames & Hudson, London, 1969, p. 186.

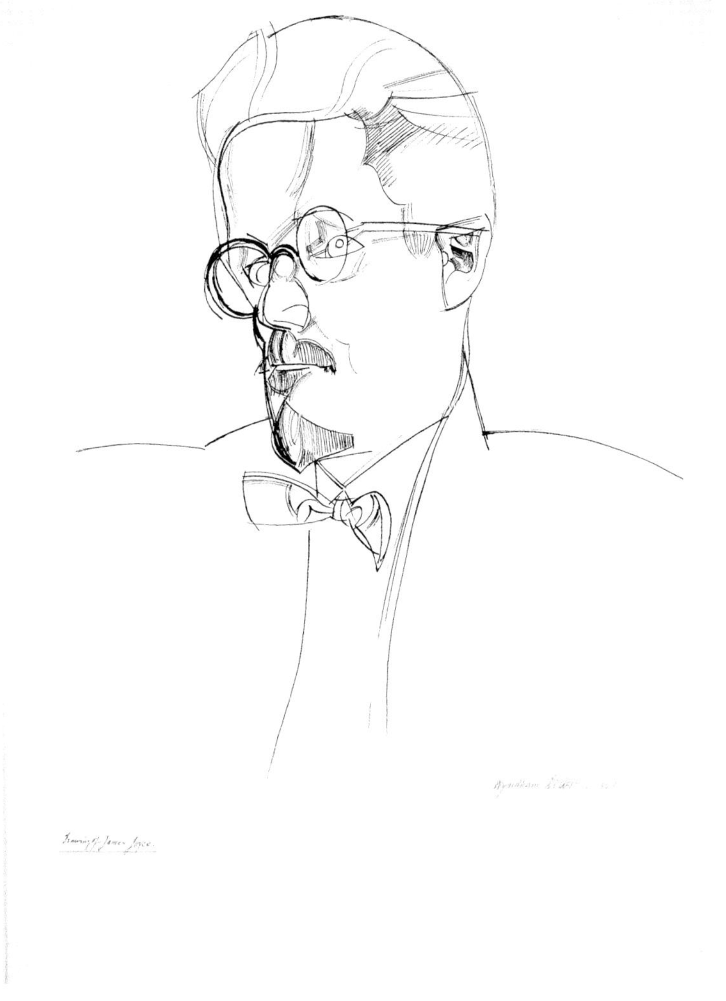

Fig 3
*James Joyce*, 1921, pen and ink on paper, 45.5 x 31.5 [M463]
National Gallery of Ireland

was now producing a series of non-fictional works of critical analysis covering political theory (Rousseau, Proudhon and Sorel), high culture, popular culture and the consumer society, philosophy (metaphysics and theology), psychology, the role of the family and gender politics. The core of this project was a group of three books, *The Art of Being Ruled* (1926), *The Lion and the Fox: The Role of the Hero in the Plays of Shakespeare* (1927) and *Time and Western Man* (1927). These are lively and, as one would expect, idiosyncratic books. They are also eccentrically organised (to the point, at times, of not being organised at all), but they are great books of lasting value. *Time and Western Man* in particular should be regarded as modernism's equivalent of Coleridge's *Biographia Literaria*. As Lewis later pointed out, one does not have to accept his conclusions to realise that the issues he discussed are crucial to modernity. But Lewis was by now in a thoroughly embattled position, mistrusted by his old allies and not really trusted as genuinely conservative by mainstream culture, despite the glee with which it greeted what it took to be his 'recantation' of avant-garde views. Anyone looking at his art could see that he had not become a traditionalist. Astonishingly, he now translated the immense polemical and analytical effort of these books into imaginative fiction, producing some of the most stylistically rebarbative prose of the century:

> She rested her forearms upon the lateral scrolls of the armchair, her trunk erect and slightly advanced, talking meanwhile. The coils in the upholstery beneath concertinaed under the familiar pressure – the rows at the head crushed especially by the massive decline of the legs, and the front portion of the roll permanently depressed .... Except for vivacious and intelligent movements of the head, she moved very little while seated. The eagerly-disputed, ruthlessly-discouraged embonpoint, though not excessive, would yet allow of no unpremeditated physical licence.[20]

The description is a literary equivalent of Lewis's drawing. The book it comes from, *The Apes of God*, satirises the emptiness of London art-life and culminates in the sham-revolution of the 1926 General Strike. Another novel, *The Childermass*,[21] depicts the unstable environment of the afterworld where two lost souls, killed in the First World War, wander desultorily before witnessing the ideological struggles at a corrupt court where a clownish, Mussolini-like official decides the fate of the dead.

Since the early 1920s Lewis had been living with Gladys Anne Hoskins (known familiarly as Froanna), who became a favourite model for his drawings after the break-up with Iris Barry. They married in 1930, but she remained resolutely in the background of his public and social life, and many of his acquaintances were unaware of her existence. Lewis is usually held responsible for this occultation, and since he lived such a compartmentalised life it probably was his doing. But this strange treatment does not reflect her importance in his subsequent life.[22] It is arguable that it was his increasing recognition of her as a person in her own right that gave his art a more humanistic turn in the 1930s. His politics, in the meantime, seemed to be headed in a contrary direction. In 1931 he visited Berlin to sell books to a German publisher. The real significance of the visit, however, was the use to which he put his observations in the book he wrote on return, *Hitler*. This sympathetic exposition of Nazism does not go so far as to recommend the system for Great Britain, but it holds out the hope that Germany, ruined by the inflation and slump of the 1920s, might recover economic prosperity by seeing off Communism and supporting Hitler. Until 1938 Lewis would remain, in what became an obsessive attention to international politics, sympathetic to the German regime, recommending friendship with it (and appeasement of it) as the best way of avoiding the war that increasingly looked inevitable.[23] A visit to Germany and Poland in 1937 caused him to relax his enthusiasm, and by 1939 he realised his errors; his inappropriately titled book from early that year, *The Jews: Are they Human?*, attacks anti-Semitism and urges the admission of Jewish refugees from the Nazis into Britain. It was highly praised

20 Wyndham Lewis, *The Apes of God* (1930), Black Sparrow Press, Santa Barbara, 1981, p. 250.

21 Wyndham Lewis, *The Childermass: Section I*, Chatto & Windus, London, 1928. Further sections were not composed until the 1950s.

22 Paul O'Keeffe notes how little is known about Mrs Lewis, and speculates that she destroyed the documents from which the facts of her life and relationship with Lewis could be reconstructed: O' Keeffe, *Some Sort of Genius*, pp. 248–49.

23 See *Hitler*, Chatto &Windus, London, 1930; *Left Wings over Europe: Or, How to Make a War about Nothing*, Jonathan Cape, London, 1936; and *Count Your Dead: They are Alive! Or, A New War in the Making*, Lovat Dickson, London, 1937.

24 The title parodies a bestseller of the time by Gustaff Renier, *The English: Are they Human?* See O'Keeffe, *Some Kind of Genius*, pp. 390–91.

25 Wyndham Lewis, *The Revenge for Love* (1937), Penguin, London, 2004.

26 Wyndham Lewis, 'Super-nature versus Super-real', in *Wyndham Lewis the Artist: From 'Blast' to Burlington House*, Laidlaw & Laidlaw, London, 1939, p. 64.

by the *Jewish Chronicle*.[24] Initially, Lewis had regarded Nazi anti-Semitism as a minor matter that should not distract from the great issue of peace or war, a position all the more comfortable for him since some of his own work had expressed or implied anti-Semitic views.

For Lewis the 1930s were a time not only of damaging political obsession. Between 1933 and 1937 he underwent a series of operations for bladder infections that he was fortunate to survive. He was also beset with legal problems, as people queued up (it seemed) to assert that they had been libelled in his books. Nevertheless he managed to publish sixteen books during the 1930s, including two novels, one of which, *The Revenge for Love* of 1937, he regarded, with some justice, as his best.[25] He also began to resume his career as a visual artist, beginning with a series of 30 portrait heads in pencil in 1932. His draughtsmanship in the 1930s lost its exciting but slightly inhuman incisiveness and was allowed to respond more generously to nature. The drawings of his wife's dog, or the *Berber Boy* (cat. 29, 30 and 27), exemplify this. Lewis scorned mere imitation, and in his return to nature attempted 'by the methods of elimination, or of simplification [to transform] the objects of nature … into something like themselves, yet differing, in reality, as much as chalk from cheese. This was the great achievement of the Orient, especially the Chinese.'[26] He mistrusted the European traditions deriving from the Renaissance, despite the origin of his own draughtsmanship within them.

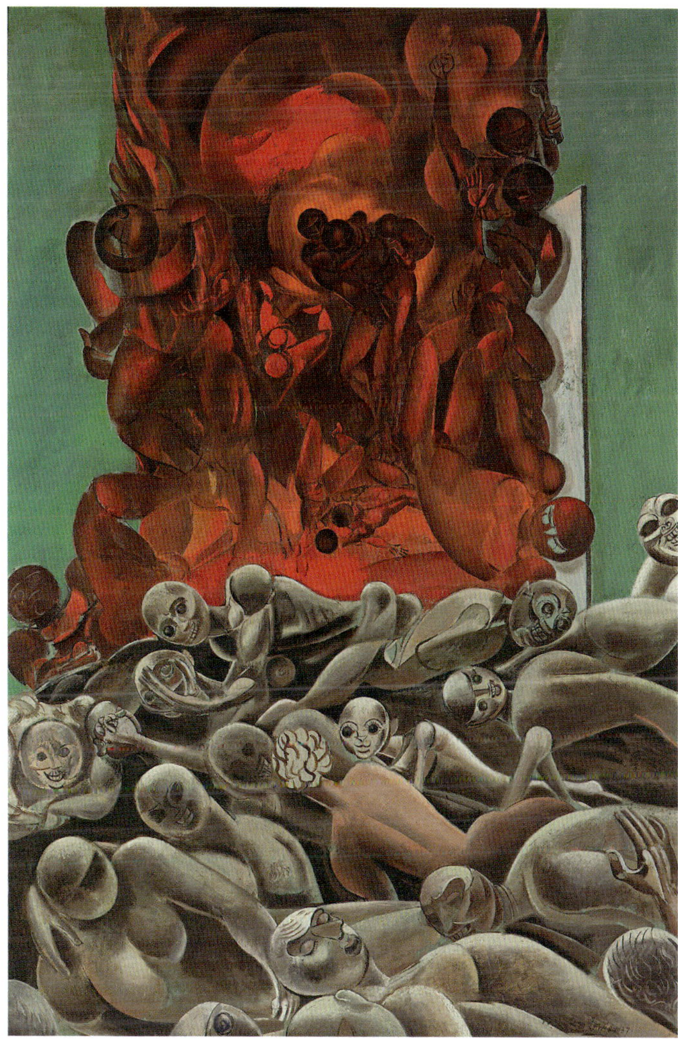

Fig. 4
*Inferno*, 1937, oil on canvas, 152.5 x 101.8 [M P72]
National Gallery of Victoria, Melbourne, Australia (Felton Bequest, 1964)

Lewis complained bitterly about a 'left-wing orthodoxy' during the 1930s, but in 1937, when he was holding an exhibition of his recent work Stephen Spender organised a letter to *The Times* urging that some work by this important painter be acquired for the nation. It was signed by (among others) Henry Moore, W.H. Auden, Serge Chermayeff, Naomi Mitchison, Rebecca West and Geoffrey Grigson. The Tate Gallery purchased *Red Scene*, one of a series of paintings (including *Inferno*, fig. 4) imagining the borderland between physical and metaphysical existence: invalids, the dead and those recuperating from sickness populate these paintings, which were clearly influenced by De Chirico and the

Surrealists. *Inferno* depicts 'a world of shapes locked in eternal conflict ... superimposed upon a world of shapes, prone in the relaxations of an uneasy sensuality which is also eternal'.[27] The shapes in conflict are muscular figures, this time quite clearly deriving from the Renaissance tradition of the heroic masculine nude, and they tumble blindly into passivity. Other 'history' paintings in the exhibition recorded, in dream vision, the tragic cycles of destructive Western energies that were about to be repeated in the forthcoming war. In the works of the 1930s, Lewis explained, it was the '*literary* imagination' that was given the freedom to invent.[28] *Four Figures in a Landscape* (cat. 34) is perhaps the closest in spirit to the work Lewis was referring to, but from this time onwards, as his eyesight gradually faded, and he relied less on virtuoso draughtsmanship, fantastic subject-matter began to predominate in his art.

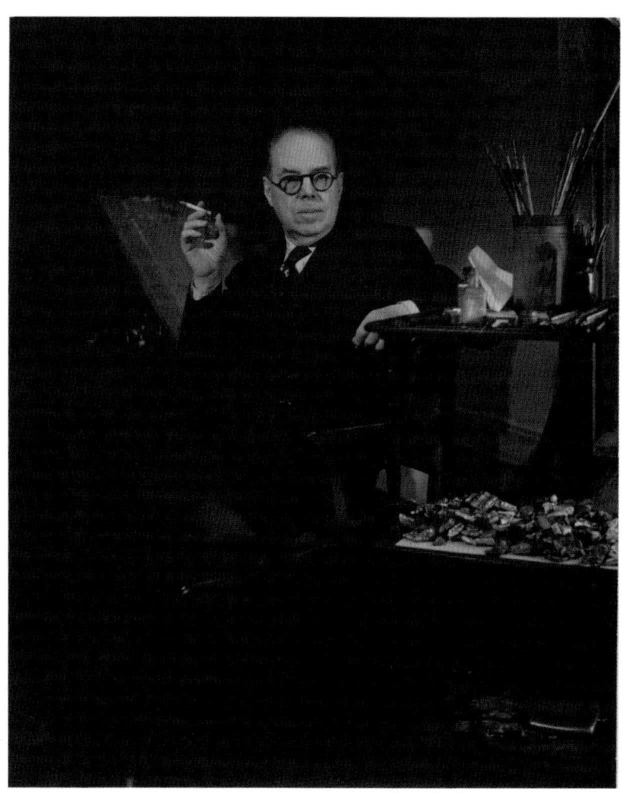

Fig. 5
Wyndham Lewis, photograph, c. 1951
Division of Rare and Manuscript Collections, Cornell University Library

One last controversy awaited him in the 1930s, however. For the first time in his life, he submitted, in 1938, a painting to the Royal Academy's annual exhibition. It was a scrupulously naturalistic portrait of T.S. Eliot, and it was rejected. Augustus John resigned in protest, editorials were written in the national press, and Lewis bombarded the correspondence columns with denunciations of the Academy's pusillanimity. Wishing to compile a series of portraits of poets, Lewis also painted Stephen Spender and Ezra Pound, but the war he had vainly hoped could be averted was declared in September 1939, and he and Froanna embarked for North America, where they would remain for the duration. Lewis expected to make a better living there than he could in England in wartime, but the stay turned into a nightmare. He seems not to have noticed that none of the nine books he had published since Hitler came to power in 1933 had been taken by an American publisher. In New York he stepped into controversy by publishing a critical article on Picasso and announcing in another piece the 'death of abstract art'. New York thought differently. Here, he really was an outsider with few friends, and those friends he had were as likely as not to be alienated by his odd behaviour. In a borrowed house in Sag Harbor, Long Island, he nevertheless completed another novel (again rejected by US publishers) before having to leave for Canada on the expiry of his visa. In Toronto he showed customary tact by publishing a light-hearted satirical account of his hosts; to his surprise they took offence.[29]

The novel that Lewis published in 1954, *Self Condemned*, is based on his and his wife's experience of an extended residence (November 1940 to May 1943) in a hotel in Toronto. It presents life in that city (or 'Momaco', as it becomes in the novel) as an ordeal by ice and fire that, thanks to the companionship of his wife, humanises its arrogant protagonist, but finally turns him into a shell of himself after she, in despair, commits suicide. Written in England after Lewis had lost his sight in 1951, the novel transposes some of his post-Second World War troubles back onto the wartime years.[30] The drawings actually made in 1941–42 show an imagination at times playful, at times tragic, that would not be confined or caged by the difficult circumstances in which he found himself. It was only in England in the 1950s, as the tumour that blinded him was growing in his skull, that the clouding of consciousness he attributes to the monotony of hotel life actually crept up on him.

Lewis's final years in London (fig. 5), despite his gradual deterioration in health, were a period of comparative success and public recognition. As the art critic of *The Listener* he was almost always positive and appreciative about the works he reviewed, especially those by young artists like Michael Ayrton, Robert Colquhoun and Francis Bacon. When he could no longer see he still continued writing, even about art, and the BBC commissioned him to complete the unfinished 1928 *Childermass*, which they then broadcast as a radio drama. Set, like the first part, in a fictional afterworld, it concerned the moral and religious imperatives facing an erring intellectual in a time of ideological upheaval, and can be seen as an imaginary autobiography. As such, it bears out Walter Michel's description of Lewis as 'a twentieth-century man, one of the last "Europeans" [whose] fractured career accurately reflects the fate of the West'.[31] The European dimension is also shown in essays on Sartre, Malraux and Camus published in 1952.

In 1956, Lewis, by now frail and unable to see his work, was finally honoured with a retrospective at the Tate Gallery, *Wyndham Lewis and Vorticism*. It was noticed that, over the previous fifty years, under cover of a noisy barrage of 'enemy salvos', an impressive visual oeuvre had come into being. When he died, less than a year later, his old friend T.S. Eliot (no doubt feeling unqualified to pronounce upon the art of painting) wrote, 'A great intellect is gone, a great modern writer is dead'. Michael Ayrton, a much younger friend fully qualified to judge Lewis as a painter, had already testified to the 'vitality and permanence' of Lewis's art, acknowledging its continuing influence on his own generation of painters. 'No one,' he declared, 'has made a more vital contribution to British art during the 20th century than Mr Wyndham Lewis'.[32] It was no more than the truth.

27 'Foreword', *Paintings and Drawings by Wyndham Lewis*, Leicester Galleries, London, 1937, in *Wyndham Lewis on Art*, p. 301.

28 Letter to Charles Handley-Read, 2 September 1949, in *Letters*, ed. Rose, p. 505.

29 'I Dine with the Warden', *America, I Presume*, Howell & Soskin, New York, 1940.

30 Wyndham Lewis, *Self Condemned*, Methuen, London, 1954.

31 Walter Michel, *Wyndham Lewis: Paintings and Drawings*, University of California Press, Berkeley and Los Angeles, 1971, p. 149.

32 Michael Ayrton, 'Foreword', *Wyndham Lewis*, Redfern Gallery, London, 1949, unpag.

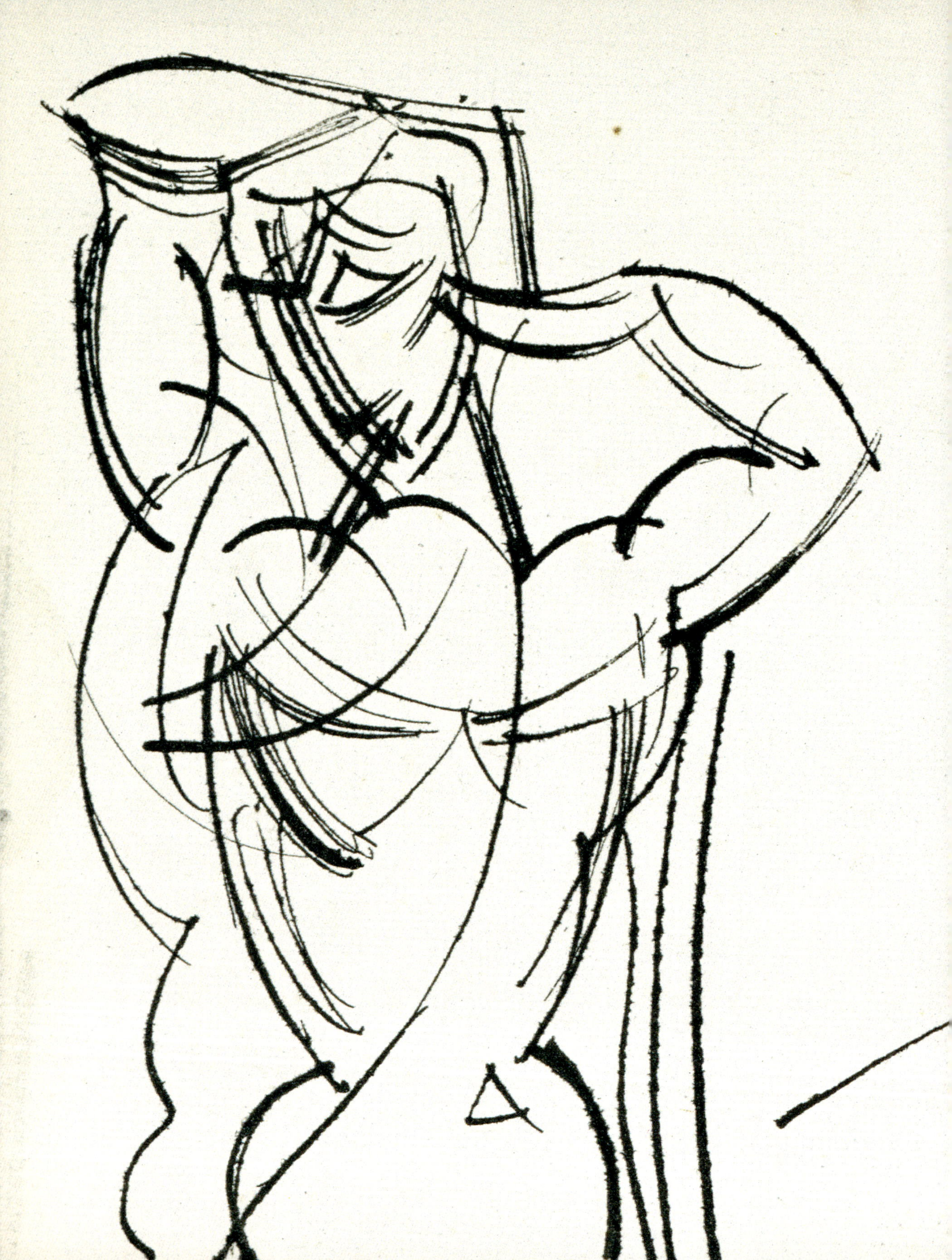

# ‘THINGS OF A MINOR KIND’? WYNDHAM LEWIS AND THE ART OF DRAWING

JACKY KLEIN

*I am an artist .... I am a novelist, painter, sculptor, philosopher, draughtsman, critic, politician, journalist, essayist, pamphleteer, all rolled into one, like one of those port manteau-men of the Italian Renaissance.*[1]

*left*
Detail from *Figures at a Beach House* (cat. 16)

By his own reckoning, Wyndham Lewis was not first and foremost a draughtsman. As the description from his 1937 autobiography shows, drawing was only one among many of his diverse occupations.[2] That painting was a more serious, publicly-oriented pursuit than drawing, and that his paintings were the more densely worked, elaborate realisations of his visual imagination, seems undisputed. Writing to the American patron John Quinn in April 1921, Lewis posited that ‘a complete painting, being more complex and on a fuller scale, has invariably the advantage over a drawing’.[3] Lewis's drawings themselves, as tangible objects, seem to suggest the same story. Often rough, sketchy, and quickly dashed off, they appear as rehearsals for the main performance – in the case of the two 1922 studies for the painting of Edwin Evans (cat. 21 and 22), quite literally so. Lewis worked rapidly, often completing a number of sketches in one sitting, re-using sheets when an initial drawing proved unsatisfactory and working, when the occasion called for it, on whatever was to hand: a cigarette packet, a British Museum reading room slip (fig. 6) or, in the case of the *Berber Boy* (cat. 27), a beer advertisement. Ephemeral fragments, Lewis's drawings, it seems, were far from treasured possessions and were often ill-cared for. When times were hard (as they often were with war raging or libels to fight) Lewis might sell 20 drawings to a dealer for just £30.[4] His apparent lack of concern, even carelessness, was noticed by his friend the poet Ezra Pound when, in 1915, he first visited Lewis's studio and was amazed at its chaotic state, with drawings strewn neglectfully around the room. Another visitor, the artist Michael Ayrton, on visiting Lewis's wife Froanna immediately after the artist's death, came just in time to rescue drawings from the Notting Hill studio, one sketch on the floor already bearing the mark of a proletarian boot’ as the flat was prepared for demolition. ‘Ayrton and his wife scooped up as many Lewis pictures as they could and bore them to safety in a laundry basket.’[5] We might well accept Lewis's own pronouncement, made in 1949 to Charles Handley-Read while he was researching his book on Lewis, that the works he had produced in between his most active bursts of productivity, drawings for the most part, were merely ‘things of a minor kind’.[6]

1 Wyndham Lewis, *Blasting and Bombardiering* (1937), Calder & Boyars, London, 1967, p. 3.

2 The reference to sculpture is typically grandiose; if Lewis sculpted, none of his works have survived.

3 Letter to John Quinn, 18 April 1921, quoted in Walter Michel, *Wyndham Lewis: Paintings and Drawings*, University of California Press, Berkeley and Los Angeles, 1971, p. 338.

4 See Walter Michel, ‘Wyndham Lewis the painter’, in *Agenda* (Wyndham Lewis Special Issue), ed. Alan Cookson, vol. 7, no. 3– vol. 8, no. 1 (3 issues), Autumn–Winter 1969–70, p. 78. Since single drawings by Lewis were often valued between £20 and £30 during and just after the First World War, this represents a very low sum; see Michel, *Paintings and Drawings*, Appendix I and II

5 C.J. Fox, notes c. 2002, Courtauld Institute of Art Gallery archive.

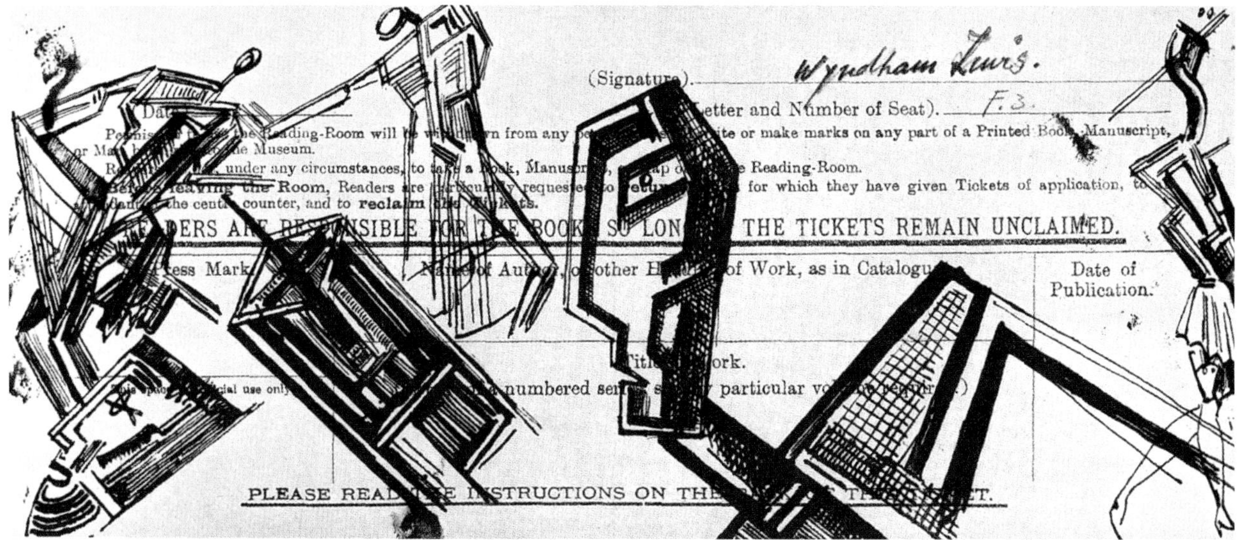


Fig. 6
*Reading Room*, 1915, pen and ink on paper, 9.5 × 22.5 [M209]
Merrill C. Berman collection

And yet drawing had been at the very heart of Lewis's early development as an artist. In 1898, before his departure from Rugby School following the discovery that Lewis was using his study as an artist's studio, arrangements were made for him 'to have special instruction in drawing several times a week. An old Scot, a beautiful silver moustache shading his red lips, gargled away at me in a Glasgow accent, but gave me much practice in the portrayal of plaster casts, and provided me with reports of unrestrained enthusiasm'.[7] So began a classical training that would continue more intensively at the Slade, under the triumvirate of Professors Fred Brown, Philip Wilson Steer and Henry Tonks but where, according to Lewis, the real 'guiding spirit and policy-maker' was the drawing instructor:

> Everything in the place was in the 'grand manner': for Professor Tonks … had one great canon of draughtsmanship, and that was the giants of the Renaissance. Everyone was attempting to be a giant and please Tonks. None pleased Tonks – none, in their work, bore the least resemblance to Michelangelo. The ladies went upstairs and wept when he sneered at their efforts to become Giantesses.[8]

Dutiful and precise study from sculptures, casts and the nude was Tonks's preferred method, combined with regular stints of copying from the Old Masters in the British Museum print room, a discipline which brought Lewis into direct contact with the revered Michelangelo, as well as Raphael, Leonardo, Luca Signorelli (who became a personal favourite to emulate) and other 'shrines of the cinquecento'.[9] It was through these trips to the British Museum that he also first came into contact with non-western art, passing through the galleries of African, Oceanic and Oriental objects, surreptitiously sketching Pacific Island masks and developing deeper interests, such as an appreciation for Chinese art.

Lewis's abilities as a draughtsman were recognised by his teachers and in 1900 he was awarded a Slade scholarship. Ability was not enough, however, and he was dismissed from the Slade prematurely in 1901 for his poor attendance and rebellious attitude. His training continued informally, however, when he travelled to Spain the following year with his friend Spencer Gore and the two young artists copied the work of Velazquez and Goya. After a spell in Paris Lewis departed for Haarlem, where by October 1904 he was studying the work of Frans Hals – this, perhaps, an attempt to master the Northern European tradition which he felt he had failed to do a few years earlier when students at the Slade were eagerly following the example of Augustus John in the rage for Rembrandt.

While Lewis came to disavow both the Slade and the Old Masters, 'blasting' Tonks in the first issue of his Vorticist journal and labelling Michelangelo his *bête noire*, he could hardly deny the importance that this early training had had on his development as an artist. Most telling are the drawings produced in a fit of creative brilliance after the First World War when, in a radical change of direction, Lewis began a series of studies from the figure, going about his work in a decidedly academic, 'Tonksian' manner, albeit now in an entirely new idiom of taut and stylised pencil and ink strokes that would have scandalised his former teacher (*Reclining Nude*, cat. 15).

So it is unsurprising, given the centrality of drawing in Lewis's artistic training, that it is through his drawings that we can best recreate his earliest artistic impulses. This is all the more so when we recognise that the first major oil painting of Lewis's to survive is the 1914–15 canvas *The Crowd.*[10] Drawings like *Alfred de Pass* (?) (cat. 1) and *Two Nudes* (cat. 2) of around 1903, the important group of satirical works from 1912 including *Two Muscular Figures* (cat. 9), *Post Jazz* (cat. 10) and *Figure in Profile* (cat. 8) and the prototype Vorticist compositions such as *Figure (Spanish Woman)* (cat. 5) thus take on a particular significance within the body of Lewis's early work. The sole survivors of his youthful imaginings, the visual counterparts of his major early literary endeavours like *Tarr* and *The Wild Body* stories, these drawings become the essential lifeline to Lewis's visual world, the vital 'documents' of his nascent career. And this career, intriguingly, was one which according to Lewis 'began at about the age of eight' with drawings to illustrate his first books. In *Rude Assignment*, published in 1950, the last of his autobiography-cum-social-critiques, he describes these 'stiff and hieratic friezes … long chains of matchstick-men – Klee-men – each trailing a musket or grasping, in a hand like a bomb, a hatchet, [which] went right across the double page.'[11] Lewis saw this first work as a landmark in his career, his claim to an early accomplishment at drawing echoing that of generations of artists, Picasso among them, for a prodigious childhood talent. Like Picasso, Lewis was engaged in a form of mythologising and, through the suggestion of his precocious skill as a draughtsman, was establishing drawing at the very root of his creative persona.

If drawing was central to Lewis's early artistic identity and his sense of mythic status as a modernist, it continued to be so in later life. In 1913, following pro-

6 Letter to Charles Handley-Read, 12 August 1949, in *The Letters of Wyndham Lewis*, ed. W.K. Rose, Methuen, London, 1963, p. 503.

7 Wyndham Lewis, *Rude Assignment: A Narrative of My Career up-to-date*, Hutchinson, London, 1950, p. 111.

8 *Ibid.*, pp. 111 and 119.

9 Letter to James Thrall Soby, 9 April 1947, in *Letters*, ed. Rose, p. 407.

10 *The Crowd*, 1914–15, oil on canvas, Tate, London. A number of major early paintings were either lost or destroyed, including *Port de Mer*, 1911, *Kermesse*, 1912, *The Laughing Woman*, 1913, *Christopher Columbus*, 1914, and *Plan of War*, 1914.

11 *Rude Assignment*, p. 110.

duction problems which halted an intended illustrated edition of Shakespeare's *Timon of Athens*, Lewis used the completed watercolours instead to produce a portfolio of drawings which he offered for sale through his fictional publishing house, The Cube Press (see cat. 6). Another similar venture came in 1919 through a collaboration with his friend, the poet John Rodker, with the production through Rodker's Ovid Press of a portfolio of reproductions entitled *Fifteen Drawings*. Here Lewis included examples of both his most recent work from the nude and his finest satiric drawings from the pre-war period, including among them *Post Jazz* (cat. 10). A third and final portfolio of drawings came out in the wake of Lewis's exhibition at the Lefevre Galleries in October 1932, *Thirty Personalities*. The portfolio, *Thirty Personalities and a Self-portrait*, was published in November of the same year by Desmond Harmsworth, nephew of the press baron Lord Rothermere and himself one of the 'personalities'. The portfolios were not produced in mass number and their prices hardly suggest that they were intended for anything but the specialist audience; indeed a letter from Lewis to Rodker in June 1919, congratulating the publisher on a similar portfolio of drawings by Henri Gaudier-Brzeska, passed on to Lewis by Edward Wadsworth, suggests that such editions at least in part served a professional audience, as artists used them to keep up to date with one another's work.[12] Their significance lies rather in the degree to which Lewis saw his drawings as status objects within his oeuvre, capable of accurately representing his artistic vision to the public, albeit a limited one. The mainly pen and ink or pencil drawings he chose for reproduction were undoubtedly works that would reproduce well, where the darker or more textured surfaces of oil paintings might not. But intriguingly the works selected were not just drawings of a type one might consider 'finished'. Some, like *Post Jazz*, employed delicate washes and were ethereal and seemingly spontaneous. The portfolio even included the apparently throw-away *Reading Room*, the 1915 drawing on the British Museum requisition slip with its coterie of half-mechanised, half-human forms. Such works, it seems, were hardly the scraps they might at first appear.

Portfolios were not the only type of publication in which Lewis chose to reproduce his drawings. In almost all of his numerous journals, autobiographies, writings and pamphlets on his life and art, Lewis reproduced his own work, and almost always his graphic work. Both editions of *The Tyro* journal produced in 1921 and 1922, and all three of *The Enemy* published in 1927 and 1929, were illustrated with examples of Lewis's drawing. *Blasting and Bombardiering* of 1937 and *Wyndham Lewis the Artist* of 1939 were littered with reproductions of his drawing, the latter including *Spartan Portrait (Naomi Mitchison)* (cat. 32), one of a number of works which Lewis hoped would show the reader what was possible when geometry and structure underpinned drawing, when one '[buried] Euclid deep in the living flesh'.[13] And significantly, Lewis's most substantial piece of writing on the nature of drawing, an unpublished essay from the late 1930s entitled *The Role of Line in Art*, was intended to be reproduced with six or more coloured drawings, all of which were to be by Lewis himself.[14]

The presence of drawings in Lewis's lifetime exhibitions also points to their

12 Letter to Rodker, 1 June 1919, in *Letters*, ed. Rose, p. 105. *Timon of Athens* sold for 10s. 6d but the number of copies produced is unknown; *Fifteen Drawings* was produced in an edition of 250 (although perhaps as few as 50 were issued) and sold at two guineas, later reduced to £2 net; *Thirty Personalities and a Self-portrait* was in an edition of 200 and sold for two guineas.

13 'Super-nature versus Super-real', in *Wyndham Lewis the Artist: From 'Blast' to Burlington House* (1939), Haskell House, New York, 1971, p. 59.

14 Wyndham Lewis, *The Role of Line in Art*, privately printed by Cameron McWhirter, New York, 1992. The production of this essay was arrested by the onset of the Second World War and the death of the publisher, George Viscount Carlow, in 1944.

key importance in the public presentation of his art. In all of his major solo exhibitions, from the 1919 exhibition *Guns* at the Goupil Gallery to the final retrospective show at the Tate Gallery in 1956, *Wyndham Lewis and Vorticism*, drawings were a key feature of the displays, and at times the prime focus of the shows. Indeed at most of the exhibitions drawings vastly outnumbered paintings on the walls of the gallery, in defiance of the usual practice where they might have been relegated to a small adjoining space and seen as a complement to the works in oil.[15] Similarly he chose drawings to submit to many of the most important mixed exhibitions of the 1910s and '20s, including the Second Post-Impressionist Exhibition at the Grafton Galleries from October to December 1912, where he showed eight drawings including six of the *Timon* series, the first London Group exhibition in March 1914 at the Goupil Gallery, the first Vorticist group show at the Doré Galleries in June 1915 and Group X's only show, in 1920 at the Mansard Gallery, where five works were shown, four of them drawings. It is little surprise when we consider that Lewis produced over a thousand drawings in his lifetime, compared to only around a hundred paintings. And yet it signals a pronounced desire to show works on paper publicly, a belief that they were an integral part of his visual oeuvre. As such it suggests that there was less of a clear distinction in Lewis's mind than we might suppose between the boundaries of the drawn and painted line.

Drawings shown at exhibition tell us a certain amount, but it is the drawings produced by Lewis away from the public eye, *between* the periods of his most intense artistic creativity, that perhaps tell us most about the role of drawing in his oeuvre as a whole. The drawings fill important gaps in which Lewis was previously thought to have produced almost nothing in the way of visual art. This is the case for example in the late 1920s, where substantial coloured mixed-media drawings such as *Three Sisters* of 1927 (cat. 25), *Figures in the Air* (1927, M635, private collection) and *Wrestling* of 1929 (cat. 26) suggest his continued commitment to at least one form of artistic expression. Through periods of illness in the 1930s, particularly 1932–36 when Lewis was frequently in hospitals and nursing homes, drawing could provide the means by which to keep himself working, if only sporadically, since it required far less physical effort than did large-scale painting. And this was true too when financially Lewis was in difficulty and had neither studio space nor materials to pursue larger projects in oil. Writing to his patron Sidney Schiff in May 1933 after a bout of illness, Lewis explained how over the last decade he had been forced out of successive studios as a result of financial problems, and so had 'retired into rooms', producing 'pictures and drawings, usually small, (as in a small room it is difficult to paint a large picture)'. No doubt in a bid for further charity (Schiff had just sent him a cheque for £25), Lewis adds: 'The new work I have been completing … I have had to do on a chair, for the simple reason that I have not, since my illness, had the money to spare to buy the necessary easel', driving his point home by enumerating just how little such an item would cost.[16] Similarly, his time in America and Canada during the Second World War (fig. 7), long considered a hiatus in Lewis's working life, has recently been reassessed as a period of consistent creativity both in his

15 *Thirty Personalities* at the Lefevre Galleries in 1932, for example, was entirely a drawings exhibition, as was a show at the Adelphi Gallery in January 1920 entitled *Drawings by Wyndham Lewis*. The *Guns* exhibition was almost entirely made up of drawings, and the Redfern Gallery show in 1949, *Wyndham Lewis*, had around 100 drawings to 21 oils. For reprinted exhibition catalogues see Michel, *Paintings and Drawings*, Appendix 1, pp. 429–46. It is important to note, however, that some works were shown but not listed in catalogues, while others were either not sent or not hung.

16 Letter to Sydney Schiff, 21 May 1933, in *Letters*, ed. Rose, pp. 212–13.

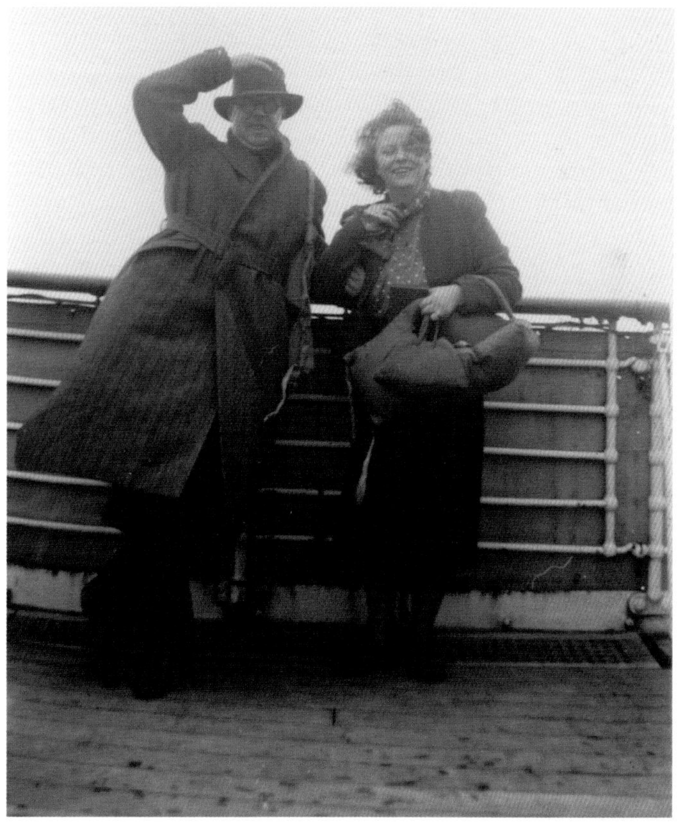

Fig. 7
Wyndham and Gladys Anne Lewis, probably on board *The Empress of Britain* en route to Canada, September 1939
Division of Rare and Manuscript Collections, Cornell University Library

writing and his art.[17] The best of the drawings from this period, particularly the group of watercolours from 1941–42 which include *A Man's Forms falling from a Small Horse* (cat. 45), *Lebensraum II: The Empty Tunic* (cat. 48) and *Creation Myth* (cat. 49), in fact provide eloquent testimony to Lewis's visual originality in their eccentric subject-matter, arcane iconography and technical dexterity. Lewis recognised their significance even as he was working on them, writing in November 1941 to the Director of the Museum of Modern Art in New York, Alfred H. Barr, about the important drawings he had produced that year and urging Barr, though unsuccessfully, to make a purchase.[18]

When we consider that some of the most worked-up and 'painterly' of the coloured drawings come at these periods when painting was near-impossible for Lewis, either creatively or logistically, it begins to appear that drawing functioned, in a sense, *as* painting for Lewis. Indeed, on at least one occasion a drawing, *Women* of 1922 (cat. 23), was actually mistaken for an oil when it was reproduced.[19] The drawings stand as substitutes for paintings when means, materials or the creative will was not there, or at times when Lewis was so taken up with his written work, as in much of the 1920s and '30s, that more significant production would have been unfeasible. Of critical importance, as Lewis reminded the reader in *Rude Assignment*, was that 'If I did not exhibit pictures it did not mean that I was unproductive'.[20] The image of the young radical Vorticist who essentially disappeared from the artistic scene after the early 1920s, only to produce work in fits and spurts around the occasional exhibition, is thus challenged by the continuity of his production in drawing. Even after the onset of blindness began affecting Lewis's ability to take portrait commissions and work on large-scale oils at the end of the 1940s, the presence of dynamic and vital late works such as *The Nativity* of 1949 (cat. 52) and *Red Figures carrying Babies and visiting Graves* (cat. 53) attests to the significance of drawing in filling vital gaps in our understanding of Lewis's artistic production, a production that in fact spanned nearly half a century.

It is these lesser-known, later works that also show Lewis as an unusual and inventive colourist. Yet hand in hand with the belief that he was one of the finest draughtsmen in twentieth-century art has come an assumption that, as one early critic put it, 'The full delectable orchestra of colour ... is denied him .... He can extract all the colour he needs from a string quartette [*sic*]'.[21] It was Walter Michel who in 1969 noted that this misapprehension was largely a result of variable reproductions, mostly black and white and of poor quality, although the scarcity of exhibitions in which Lewis's finest coloured drawings have been seen – complex amalgams of vibrant watercolour, gouache, chalks and inks – has also allowed such misapprehensions to persist. It was, after all, as early as 1914 in the first edition of *Blast* that Lewis described the colour effects he was pursuing, 'exploitations of discords, odious combinations, etc... A painter like Matisse has always been harmonious, with a scale of colour pleasantly Chinese. Kandinsky at his best is much more original and bitter. But there are fields of discord untouched'.[22] And again, it is those works of the late 1930s and '40s, like *Bathing Scene* of 1938 (cat. 43), the fantasy drawings which allude to myth, literature, history and a complex personal iconography dense with political, social and sexual allusion, which make the most use of dynamic and unusual colour combinations; those pictures, as we have seen, which in their complexity and completeness might effectively function as 'paintings'. Indeed, Lewis lamented that the European word 'drawing' was wanting, inadequate to describe 'many of the greatest pictures in the world – coloured pictures, though not oil-paintings'.[23]

The drawings thus add substantially to our understanding of Lewis's skills as a colourist, and give us a much more accurate picture of his oeuvre as a whole. Yet they also act as personal ciphers of Lewis's inner life, much of which was shielded from the outside world as a result of feuds, disagreements and his own particular paranoias. As David Rosand has argued, drawing communicates more directly than other art forms the personal visions of an artist, so that through it the artist leaves his mark, signing himself'.[24] This is clearest perhaps in the intensely personal drawings of Froanna completed in the 1930s and '40s, when she became a much-used model and a recurrent presence in the drawings. While Lewis rarely painted formal portraits of Froanna in the vein of the majestic *Red Portrait* of 1937 (illus. p. 72), she is seen again and again in rare moments of intimacy, tenderness and vulnerability, reading pensively, posing nude on a sofa (cat. 36), distractedly scanning the headlines of a newspaper for some positive indication of

17 See Catherine M. Mastin, Robert Stacey and Thomas Dilworth, *'The Talented Intruder': Wyndham Lewis in Canada, 1939–1945*, Art Gallery of Windsor, Ontario, 1992.

18 Letter to Alfred H. Barr, 24 November 1941, quoted in Catherine M. Mastin and Robert Stacey, 'Introduction', *ibid.*, p. 43.

19 James Thrall Soby, *Contemporary Painters*, Museum of Modern Art, New York, 1948, p. 119.

20 *Rude Assignment*, p. 123.

21 Eric Newton, 'Wyndham Lewis', in *The Art of Wyndham Lewis*, ed. Charles Handley-Read, Faber & Faber, London, 1951, p. 31.

22 'Orchestra of Media', in *Blast*, no. 1, in *Wyndham Lewis on Art*, p. 46.

23 *The Rule of Line in Art*, p. 1.

24 David Rosand, *Drawing Acts: Studies in Graphic Expression and Representation*, Cambridge University Press, Cambridge, 2002, p. 330.

the war's progress. Her frequent appearance in the drawings belies the covert manner in which Lewis lived his life with her, omitting to introduce her to long-standing friends for example so that John Rothenstein, an acquaintance since the early 1920s, on visiting Lewis at his Kensington Gardens studio in the late 1930s, would later recall how 'suddenly I knew that Mrs. Lewis – of whose existence I had vaguely heard – was somewhere present, concealed somewhere in the tiny studio flat'.[25] Similarly, the Lewises' black and white Sealyham dog, known affectionately as 'Mr. Tut', featured in a number of drawings of the 1930s (cat. 29 and 30), carefree and playful sketches which provide a valuable antidote to the more commonly told tale of Lewis's notorious aggression, polemic and biting satire. When Tut died in 1944, Lewis wrote to a friend that the loss of 'this small creature, which stood for all that was benevolent in the universe' had brought into relief their isolation in Canada, particularly for Froanna. 'Like the spirit of a simpler and saner time, this fragment of primitive life confided his destiny to her, and went through all the black days beside us'. Little wonder then, that his death had 'left an ugly gap'.[26] The dog's appeal went beyond the Lewises: when one of the drawings of Tut was included in the Tate's 1956 exhibition, subsequently travelling to various regional centres, a journalist at the Manchester *Evening Chronicle* urged readers not to miss 'the impudent pup… an oasis in a stormy sea'.[27]

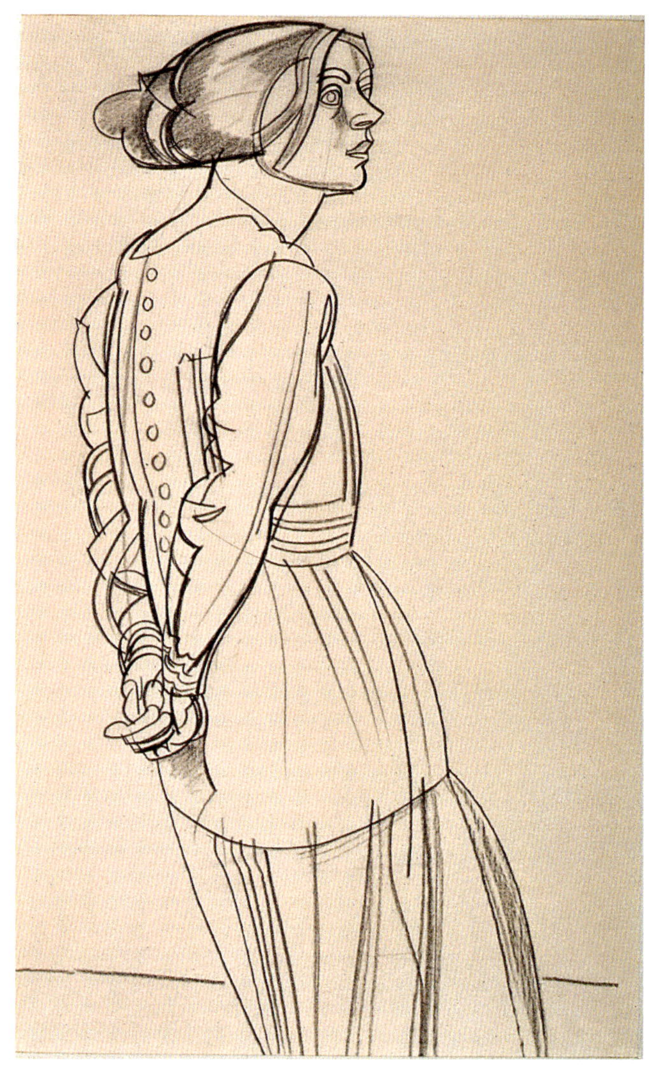

Fig. 8
*Portrait of a Girl standing*, c. 1920, crayon on paper, 42 x 26.5 [M410]
Manchester Art Gallery

It was perhaps this personal element, the spontaneity and sense of intimate communion with the artist, which made Lewis's drawings so appealing to collectors as well as critics. The coherence of Lewis's drawings as a unique and distinct body of work found favour among a number of key patrons, many of whom purposefully concentrated their acquisitions on drawings. Captain Guy Baker, with whom Lewis spent much time while sick during the First World War, was one of the earliest to recognise the significance of the drawings, collecting a now highly important group of early works dating from around 1909–17 which he bequeathed to the Victoria and Albert Museum in London on his death in 1918 during the influenza epidemic.[28] John Quinn, the noted modernist art collector, was another who saw the appeal of Lewis's work, organising and paying for the Vorticist exhibition at the Penguin Club in New York in 1917 and buying a large number of drawings, mainly under the influence of Ezra Pound, before he lost interest in the early 1920s to pursue acquisitions in contemporary French art. After his death in 1924 Quinn's works were sold in Paris in 1925 and later at the American Art Association in New York in February 1927, where 59 drawings by Lewis were listed for sale, including among them *A Masque of Timon* (cat. 6). Charles Rutherston, the brother of the artist William Rothenstein and uncle of John Rothenstein, gathered a particularly outstanding collection of drawings between December 1919 and March 1922, when Lewis was producing some of his finest pencil and pen and ink studies from life, such as *Portrait of a Girl standing* of around 1920 (fig. 8). Rutherston was a rarity as one of the few welcome visitors at Lewis's studio. 'For him I left the gate ajar… He thought nothing of buying two or three dozen designs at a time, the best of which are now in the Manchester Museum', today's Manchester Art Gallery, which inherited one important oil and 23 drawings by Lewis in 1925, along with works by notable contemporaries from Nevinson and Nash to Sickert and Bomberg.[29] Arthur Crossland of Bradford was another major patron during Lewis's lifetime, whose collection, when it came up for sale at Christie's in 1956, consisted of four paintings and 53 drawings, among them *Sea Cave* (cat. 40), *Meeting of Sheiks* (cat. 41) and *Bathing Scene* (cat. 43).[30] Finally Douglas Duncan, the collector-cum-dealer who ran the Picture Loan Society in Toronto, was a key supporter during Lewis's sojourn in Canada. Caricatured as the 'inhuman old maid' Cedric Furber in Lewis's damning 1954 novel of Canadian life, *Self Condemned*, he unsurprisingly lost touch with Lewis in later years.[31] A significant patron though during Lewis's time in Canada, he amassed some of the best of the wartime drawings, including *Creation Myth No.17* of 1941 (M968), *Witch on Cowback* of the same year (M985, both now at the National Gallery of Canada, Ottawa), and *Lebensraum II: The Empty Tunic* (cat. 48).

On his return from Canada in 1945 Lewis found employment as an occasional art critic for the BBC's *The Listener* magazine. Writing sporadically between August 1946 and May 1951 he reviewed the work of those artists, all broadly figurative, that he most admired, among them Michael Ayrton, Francis Bacon, Robert Colquhoun, Merlyn Evans, Henry Moore, John Piper, Ceri Richards and Graham Sutherland. Collectively he saw the new emerging artists as 'the finest group of painters and sculptors England has ever known'.[32] While painting was often his focus in the *Listener* articles, Lewis would never hesitate to mention a small drawings exhibition, even a single sheet worth the trip, if something particularly appealed, whether it was a geranium by Bernard Meninsky or one of the *Shelter* drawings by Henry Moore. In a regular scour 'Round the London Art Galleries' of November 1949, for example, he picked out a drawing by his former Slade role model and longtime friend Augustus John, remarking that his *Head of an Old Gypsy* (fig. 9) on view at the Lefevre Galleries 'is traditional drawing of the very highest order', indicative of how 'for John I am sure Mantegna is as contemporary as Matisse'.[33] So impressed was he that he even got the editors to reproduce the drawing for the magazine's cover. Elsewhere Lewis would use his column to expound freely on the values of good draughtsmanship and how, 'In the fine arts an understanding of good drawing is evidence of a final mastery of

25 John Rothenstein, 'Wyndham Lewis', *Modern English Painters: Lewis to Moore*, Eyre & Spottiswoode, London, 1956, p. 42.

26 Letter to Felix Giovanelli, 28 January 1944, in *Letters*, ed. Rose, pp. 376–77.

27 *Evening Chronicle*, 4 September 1956, quoted in Paul O'Keefe, *Some Sort of Genius: A Life of Wyndham Lewis*, Jonathan Cape, London, 2000, p. 623.

28 Baker left 27 drawings to the Victorian and Albert Museum. See 'Captain Guy Baker – In Memoriam', in *Blasting and Bombardiering*, pp. 207–09.

29 *Blasting and Bombardiering*, p. 219. See also Jane Farrington, 'Wyndham Lewis and a prescient collector', *Apollo*, January 1980, pp. 46–49.

30 For details of the Crossland and Quinn sales see Michel, *Paintings and Drawings*, pp. 449–50.

31 Wyndham Lewis, *Self Condemned* (1954), New Canadian Library, Toronto, 1974, p. 255. I am most grateful to Cy Fox for this reference. For more information on Duncan see *Douglas Duncan: A Memorial Portrait*, ed. Alan Jarvis, University of Toronto Press, Toronto, 1974.

32 Wyndham Lewis, *The Demon of Progress in the Arts*, Methuen, London, 1954, p. 4.

33 Wyndham Lewis, 'Round the London Art Galleries', *The Listener*, 17 November 1949, vol. 42, no 1086, p. 860.

the visual language'.[34] On occasion he would even chastise his favourite artists when he felt that their work needed a return to the basics of drawing from nature, advising Colquhoun for example in November 1950 that a stint of direct drawing from life would be a valuable corrective to his recent lack of formal density.

During the later 1940s, Lewis's own work in turn attracted the attention of a number of these younger practitioners. As Merlyn Evans wrote in a personal notebook, Colquhoun, Robert MacBryde, John Minton and Keith Vaughan were only some of the artists 'who are enjoying the beneficent influence of Wyndham Lewis'.[35] Henry Moore had for some time been an acquaintance and supporter of Lewis, signing Stephen Spender's letter to *The Times* in December 1937 along with a number of other artists and cultural figures in a bid to urge greater public recognition of his work. For Moore, Lewis provided a critical link to the generation of Epstein and Gaudier-Brzeska, and stood for a dynamism which he felt was lacking in British art. Importantly too, Lewis confirmed Moore's belief that drawing was the essential tool of any artist, including the sculptor. Even more committed a follower was Michael Ayrton. For Ayrton too, one of the vital links with Lewis was through drawing; indeed, the two men first met in the mid-1940s after Ayrton praised Lewis's draughtsmanship in his book *British Drawings*, and Ayrton himself owned a number of Lewis's works on paper, including *Young Woman seated* (cat. 37) and an important early self-portrait closely related to the proto-cubist *Self-portrait* of 1911 (cat. 3). Writing in May 1949 for the introduction to Lewis's exhibition at the Redfern Gallery, Ayrton again picked out Lewis's drawings for special praise, describing how some in the exhibition 'show Mr. Lewis's astonishing achievement as early as 1912' while 'others also exhibited ... strengthen my opinion that he is among the greatest living portraitists'.[36] Ayrton, in the role of portraitist himself, drew numerous sketches of Lewis, culminating in an oil portrait of 1955 now in the Tate collection in London. Their mutual respect also led to collaboration in the 1950s with Ayrton's dust-jacket design for *Self Condemned* and illustrations for the second and third volumes of Lewis's *The Human Age*. Even more fascinating as a gesture of collaboration, and more profound as a symbol of the centrality of drawing to their relationship, was Ayrton's re-drawing of Lewis's partially destroyed pencil study of Ezra Pound (fig. 10) in 1957. Pound's head, as other sheets of around 1919-20 suggest, had been a source of formal experimentation for Lewis, and he isolated it for particular study on a number of occasions, treating it as a separate entity from the body, often as a sort of mask.[37] Here, though, Lewis entirely cut out the head, a technique he often employed with parts of a drawing he was unhappy with. When Ayrton redrew it, he was entering Lewis's world through an engagement with draughtsmanship rather than, as had been the case with Lewis himself, an engagement with the portrait subject (Pound had in any event been incarcerated in a Washington mental asylum since 1945). As T.G. Rosenthal has noted, the drawing is 'symbolic of the real link between the two [artists] and of the influence of the older man upon the younger. For both, draughtsmanship is the great leveller'.[38]

Drawing lay at the very heart of Lewis's artistic practice, and at the core of

34 Wyndham Lewis, 'The London Art Galleries', *The Listener*, 9 June 1949, vol. 41, no. 1063, p. 988.

35 Merlyn Evans, notebook, undated, Tate Gallery Archive, TGA 896.1.7.2, p. 8A.

36 Michael Ayrton, 'Foreword', *Wyndham Lewis*, Redfern Gallery, London, 1949, unpag.

37 See Paul Edwards, *Wyndham Lewis: Painter and Writer*, Yale University Press, New Haven and London, 2000, pp. 244–46.

38 T.G. Rosenthal, 'Introduction', in *Word and Image I & II: Wyndham Lewis and Michael Ayrton*, National Book League, London, 1971, p. 5.

39 *The Role of Line in Art*, pp. 5 and 2.

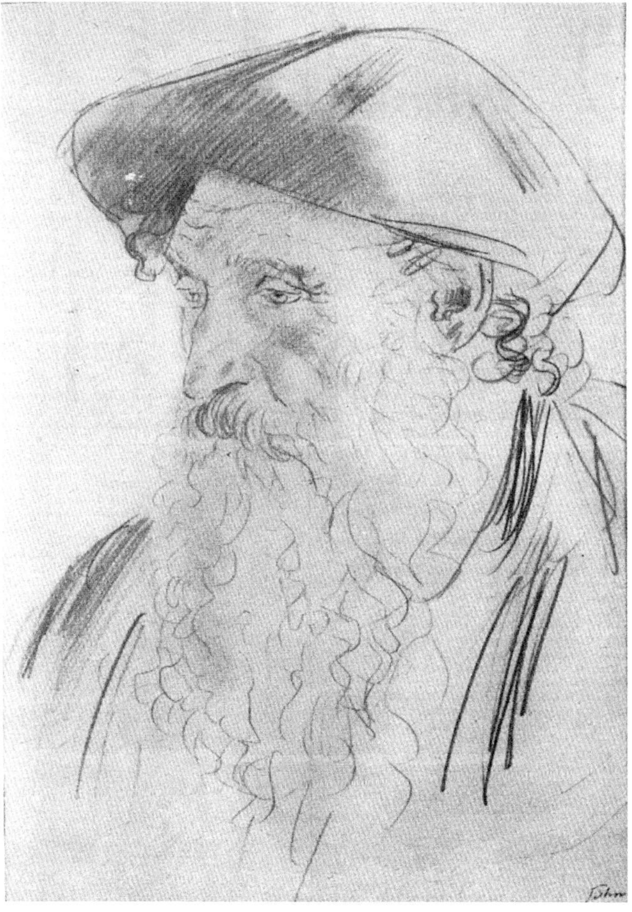

Fig. 9
Augustus John (1878–1961), *Head of an Old Gypsy*, c. 1905, medium, dimensions and location unknown


his identity as an artist. Expressing his sentiments about the centrality of draughtsmanship in his essay *The Role of Line in Art*, he described how drawing, taken in its widest sense to mean 'with burin, pen, brush, or pencil', was indeed, as Ingres had suggested, the 'probity' or integrity of art. 'It is quite true,' Lewis wrote, that 'the fine draughtsman, like the honest man, is rarely met with … it is more difficult upon a piece of white paper, your means of expression reduced to a few lines, to deceive the expert spectator than it is with a lot of oil paint upon a canvas.'[39] It was because of the inevitable 'truth' of drawing, he felt, that it was easy to identify the faults of the Impressionists and their more recent followers, who had been so reprehensible in their attempts to capture fleeting effects of nature, allowing for a slovenly approach to linear design and letting nature's transitory effects dominate. Thus drawing became key to Lewis's whole critique of the 'amateur world' of art in England as he perceived it, since it was a fundamental lack of skill in line that had begun the slippery slope to artistic mediocrity. What Lewis called for, conversely, was for artists to take control of nature.

Fig. 10
*Ezra Pound*, 1920, with the head re-drawn by Michael Ayrton (1921–75), 1957, pencil on paper, 35.5 x 51 [M413]
Private collection


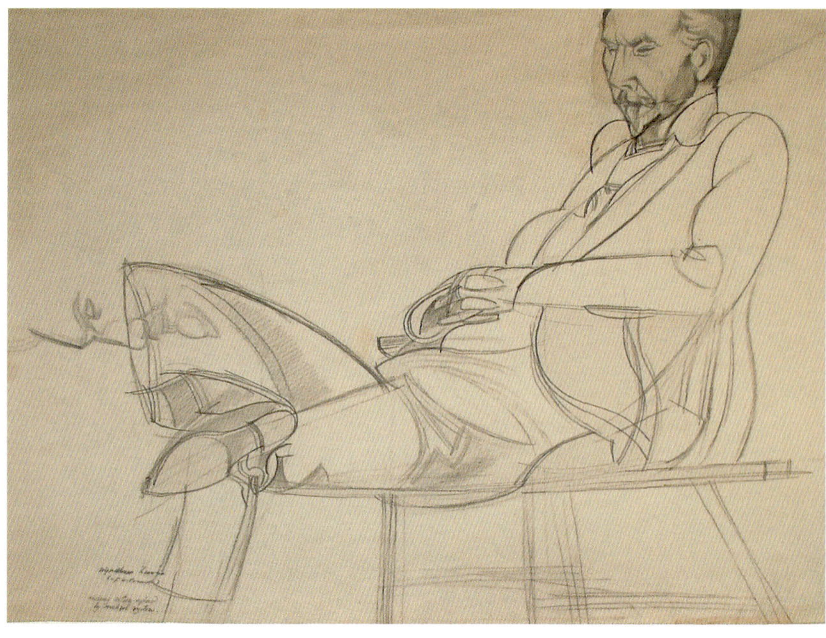

'You may dominate your visual milieu – discipline it, and legislate for it,' he directed, for 'Line implies mastery'.[40] As Tom Normand has suggested, this desire for domination can be read as a signifier for Lewis's political concerns, never far from the surface of his artistic or literary work: among them, his steadfast commitment to the idea of an ordered, stable and fixed world where the artist would be, as he was not in the real world, an empowered status figure in society.[41]

Drawing is central too for understanding the full scope of Lewis's visual oeuvre. It was during his period of intense studies from life after the First World War, his going 'underground' as he would later describe it, that a quiet revolution took place, profound and far-reaching if less bombastic than the revolution of the *Blast* years. He consistently included drawings as significant objects in their own right in his exhibitions, and produced portfolios which were intended to make clear statements about his artistic beliefs and, in the case of *Fifteen Drawings*, his dexterity as an artist. Drawing sustained Lewis at those times between his public exhibitions, when behind closed doors he persisted in making sketches when painting became practically too cumbersome or creatively too demanding; or, more simply, when the allure of a clean sheet of white paper became irresistible. Even in the most bizarre of the fantasy works from the 1930s and '40's, studies from life remained essential, the linguistic building blocks that he used to create new and fantastical languages of form.

In *The Role of Line in Art*, years after his formal training at the Slade, Lewis revisited those masters of line whose work he found most exhilarating, among them the ancient Greek vase-painters, Mantegna, Leonardo, Dürer, Goya, the

40 *Ibid*., pp. 6–7.

41 Tom Normand, *Wyndham Lewis the Artist: Holding the Mirror up to Politics*, Cambridge University Press, Cambridge, 1992, p. 152. Normand also convincingly argues that Lewis's desire to dominate is apparent in the *Thirty Personalities* drawings, where the 'capturing' of his sitters through line symbolises his attempts to win a personal battle of wills.

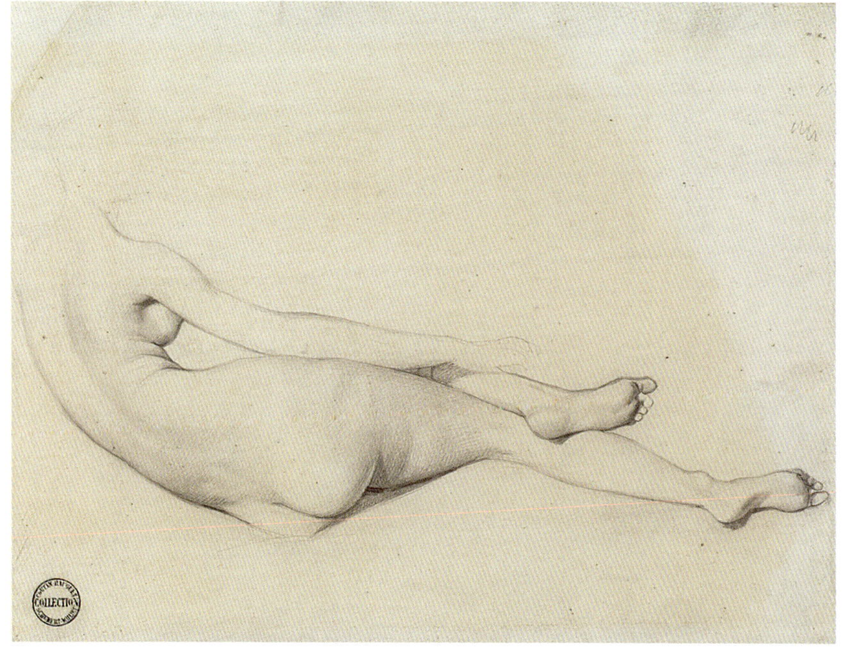

Fig. 11
Jean-Auguste-Dominique Ingres (1780–1867), *Study for La Grande Odalisque*, c. 1813–14, graphite on paper, 18.5 × 25.4
The Samuel Courtauld Trust, Courtauld Institute of Art Gallery, London

Chinese brush-masters, Degas, Picasso and Ingres (fig. 11). Yet where Ingres was unmasking the nude, exposing in her sinuous pencil curves the sensuality of French nineteenth-century desire, Lewis was always stripping away further. For him, the line was in fact nothing less than 'the bone beneath the pulp'.[42] As Lewis knew, after all, drawings communicated an immediacy that could not be disguised. Unadorned, naked, devoid of the layers of obfuscation which oil paint provided, they offered up the clearest statements of the artist's true spirit. If for Lewis line represented the essence, the bones of a work, then his drawings must form the structural backbone of his own artistic production.

42 *The Role of Line in Art*, p. 4.

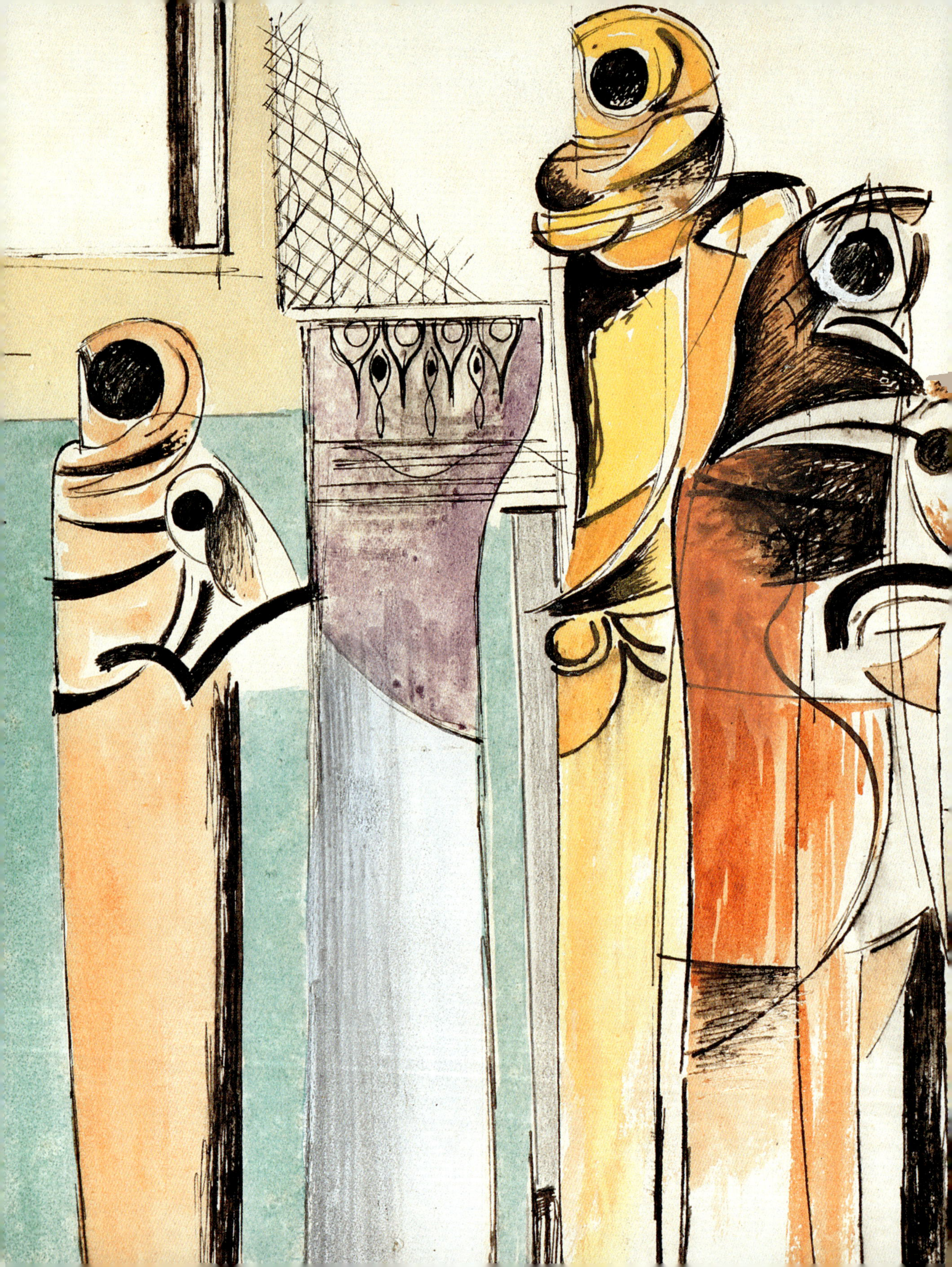

# CATALOGUE

## LUCY ASKEW AND JACKY KLEIN

This is a full catalogue of the exhibition. All dimensions are in centimetres, height before width. 'M' numbers refer to Walter Michel, *Wyndham Lewis: Paintings and Drawings*, University of California Press, Berkeley and Los Angeles, 1971. Only inscriptions in the artist's hand have been cited. Exhibition details are given only when works could be definitively identified.

*left*
Detail of *Meeting of Sheiks* (cat. 41)

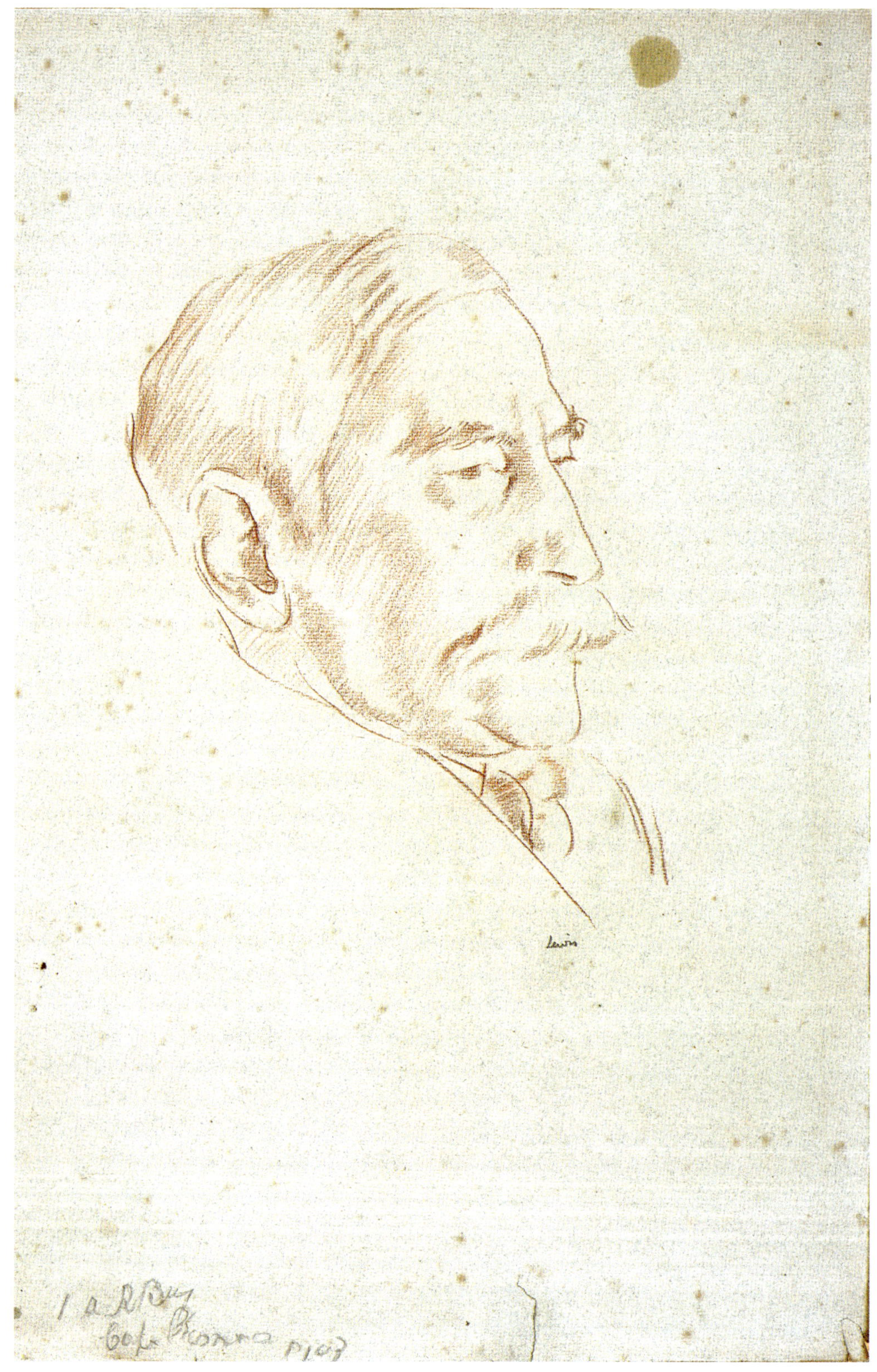

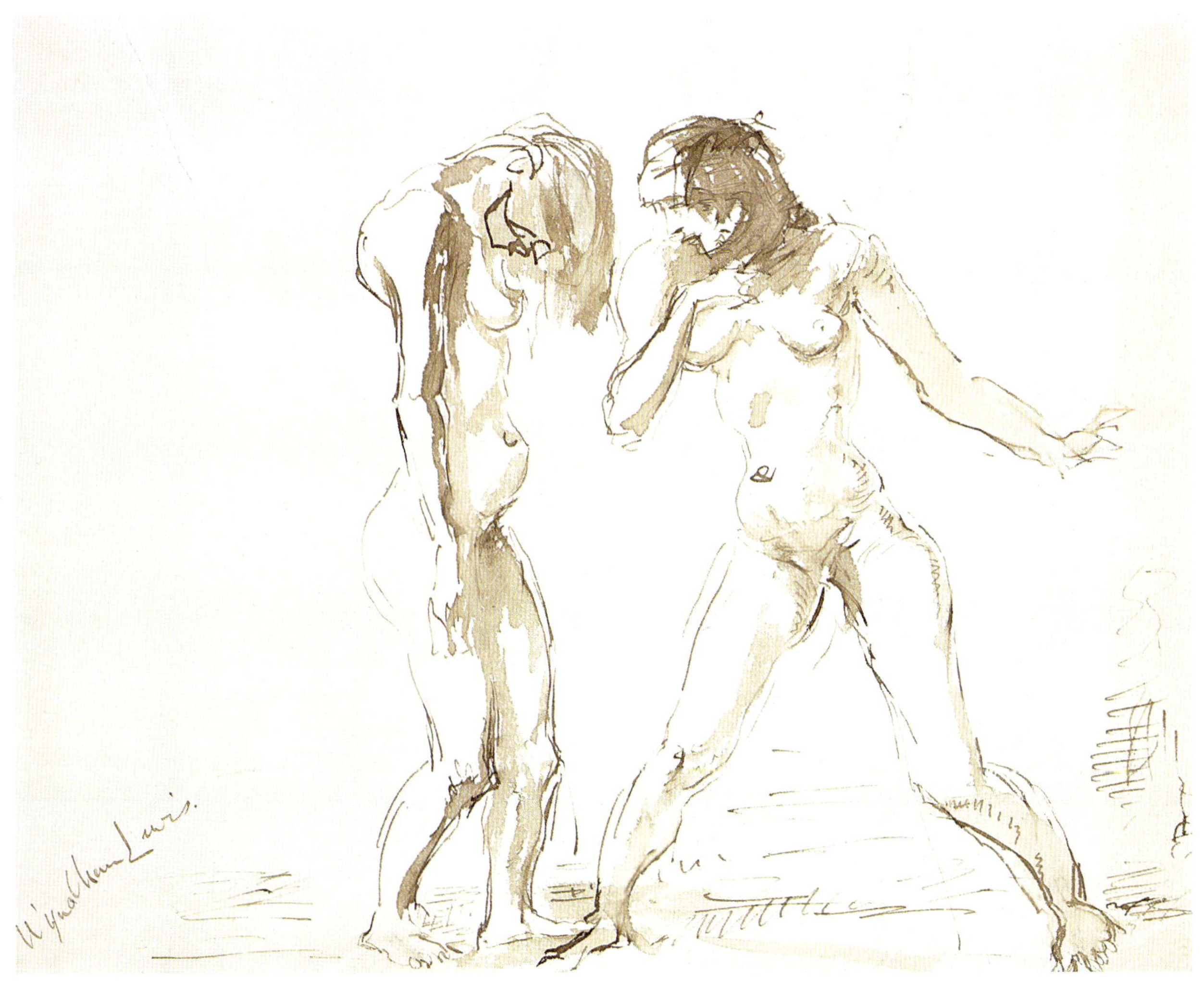


1 **ALFRED DE PASS (?) c. 1903**

Chalk on paper, 46.8 × 31
INSCRIPTIONS 'Lewis'
Wyndham Lewis Memorial Trust

2 **TWO NUDES 1903**

Pen and ink and ink wash on paper, 24.4 × 39.5 (full sheet); 21.3 × 29.5 (as shown) [M6]
INSCRIPTIONS 'Wyndham Lewis.'
EXHIBITED *Wyndham Lewis and Vorticism*, Tate Gallery, London, 1956, no. 3 (and on tour as an Arts Council Circulating Exhibition: City Art Gallery, Manchester; The Art Gallery, Glasgow; City Art Gallery, Bristol; City Art Gallery, Leeds, no. 2)
Private collection

These two drawings of around 1903 are rare examples of Wyndham Lewis's earliest known works and show the influence of Augustus John in both subject-matter and technique. The portrait is thought to be of Alfred de Pass (1861–1953), a wealthy South African collector and businessman whom Lewis may have met through his friendship with John.

## 3 SELF-PORTRAIT 1911

Pencil, watercolour and gouache on paper, 31.3 x 24.3 [M26]
INSCRIPTIONS 'W. Lewis.'; *verso*: 'Self-portrait (about 1912)' and 'W.L.'
EXHIBITED *Wyndham Lewis*, Manchester City Art Gallery, Manchester, 1980, no. 8
Wyndham Lewis Memorial Trust: Fox collection

This arresting self-portrait drawing is one of three which Lewis produced in 1911–12. While Lewis later inscribed 'about 1912' on the reverse, it is thought for stylistic reasons to have been made the previous year, when the angular forms and strong linear structure of Cubism began to enter Lewis's work. The First Post-Impressionist Exhibition, organised by Roger Fry in November 1910, had introduced Lewis to the work of Cézanne, Picasso, Derain and others, and his own art from 1911 showed the influence of these continental stylistic developments. Of his early Cubist works, and the more developed Vorticist experiments of 1913–14, Lewis later wrote, 'It was more than just picture-making: one was manufacturing fresh eyes for people, and fresh souls to go with the eyes'.[1]

In its tone, this self-portrait asserts a more openly aggressive stance and strikes a darker note than the comic and satiric works which Lewis had most recently been producing, such as *The Theatre Manager* of 1909 (M15, Victoria and Albert Museum, London). While the subtle skin tones on the cheek, nose and forehead give him a youthful, full-faced appearance, the triangular eyes set in darkened rectangular patches, and the deep shadow created by the intense light shining from the right, hint at something more sinister. At the time of this self-portrait Lewis was in his late twenties and was in the midst of writing his first novel, *Tarr*, set in bohemian Paris. While he was renowned in his youth primarily as a poet, his brash and confrontational posture here, executed in consciously avant-garde style, seems to have been an attempt to assert his emerging identity as a visual artist. Depicting himself as a solitary figure emerging from the hazy void, Lewis also makes a subtle statement about the role of the individual. In contrast to the groups of unthinking, passion-driven primitives which had occupied him in recent years, Lewis shows himself here as a lone figure, eyes open and intellectually alert.

Lewis's piercing stare was not simply affected for these self-portraits, however. Shortly after the drawing was purchased from Lewis's wife Froanna in 1965, she wrote to its new owner, C. J. Fox: 'I am pleased you are enjoying the Cubist portrait. I know so well that glare. When puzzling over some problem my eyes would absentmindedly wander around and suddenly encounter that stare which always made me pause … one can never say Wyndham ever flattered himself'.[2] The three self-portrait drawings together suggest something of the public persona which Lewis wanted to project at this time, combative and antagonistic. Writing about intellectual egos, he would later comment: 'It has been my experience of my few very eminent contemporaries that, after their various fashions, they have been the possessors of abnormally aggressive egos (and I daresay they may have discovered the same symptoms in myself)'.[3]

The pock-marked surface of this drawing, with small holes and nicks, is probably a result of damage sustained during the Second World War. The self-portrait appears to have been left in London during Lewis's sojourn in America and Canada between 1939 and 1945, surviving the war despite bomb damage to the Lewises' Notting Hill apartment. JK

NOTES

1 Wyndham Lewis, *Rude Assignment: A Narrative of my Career up-to-date*, Hutchinson, London, 1950, p. 125.
2 C.J. Fox, notes *c.* 2002, Courtauld Institute of Art Gallery archive.
3 *Rude Assignment*, p. 115.

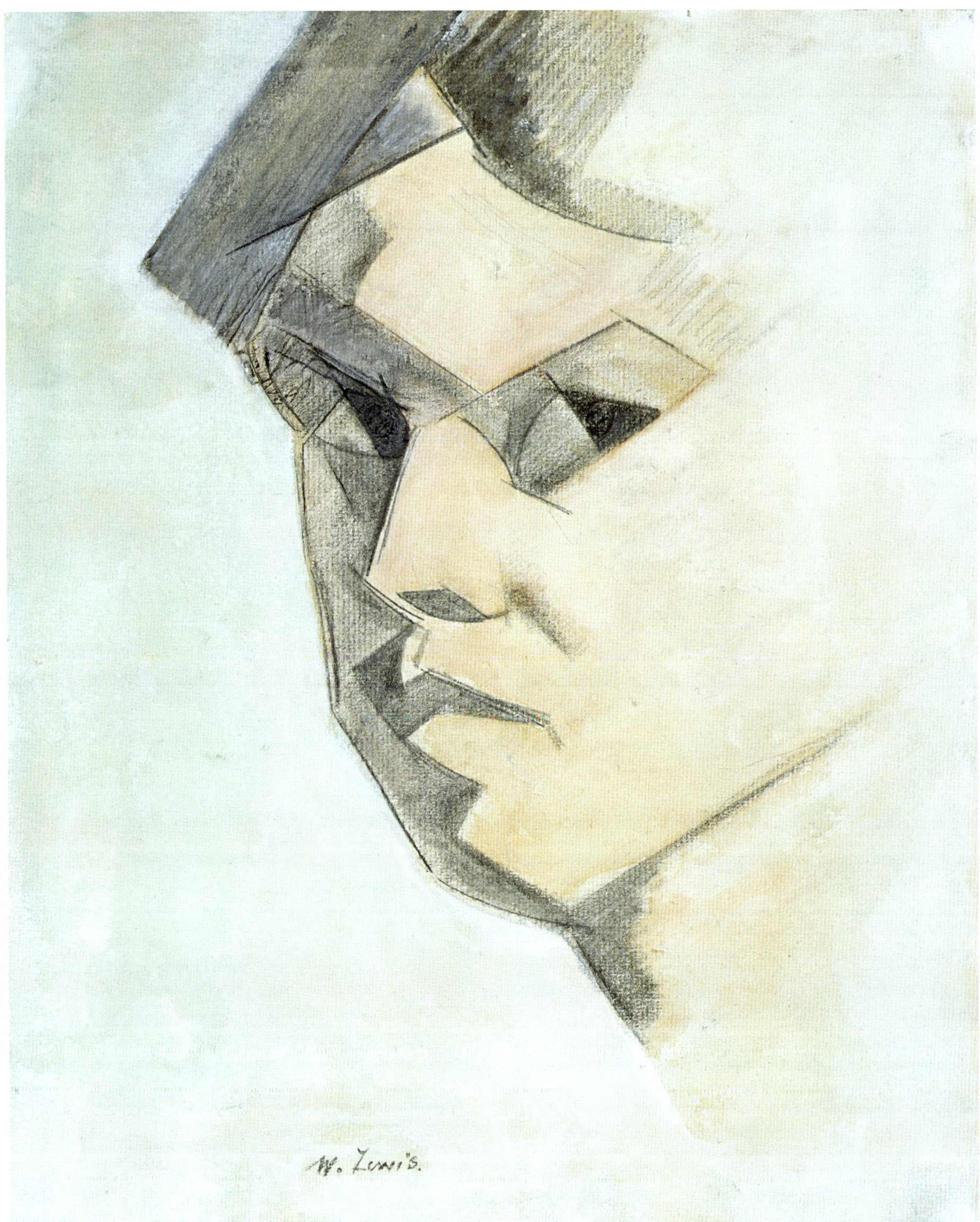
W. Lewis.

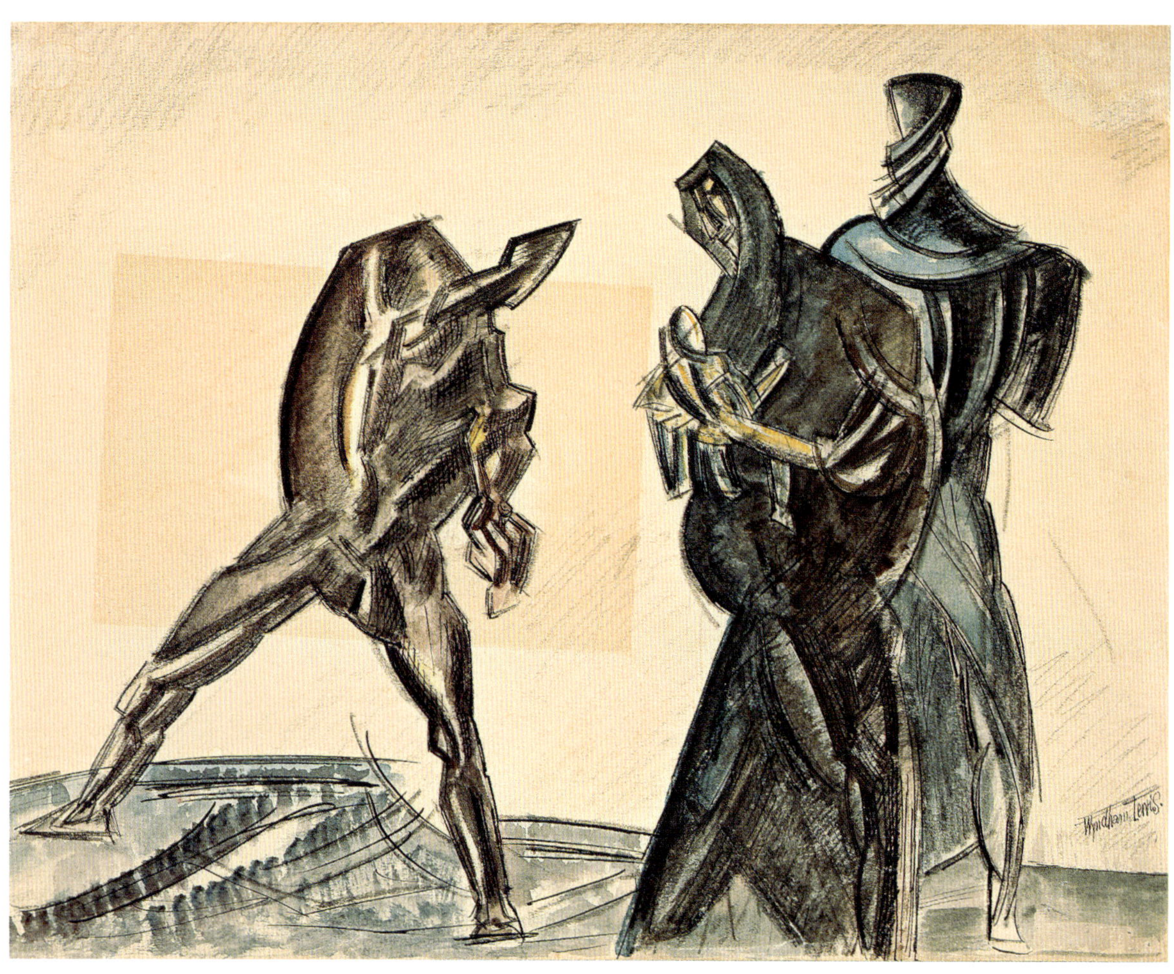


4 **FAMILY AND FIGURE 1912**

Pencil, pen and ink and watercolour on paper, 25.5 x 32.7 [M57]
INSCRIPTIONS 'Wyndham Lewis.'
Private collection

5 **FIGURE (SPANISH WOMAN) 1912**

Pen and ink and gouache on paper, 31.2 x 20.7 [M65]
INSCRIPTIONS 'Wyndham Lewis. 1912.'
Wyndham Lewis Memorial Trust: G. and V. Lane collection

The figure's striking pose and the suggestion of a traditional mantilla identify this as a Spanish woman, possibly a dancer. Lewis appears to have amended the drawing by covering the right-hand segment in gouache, accentuating the sweeping arc of the woman's back and headdress. The blue ink with which he highlighted the figure's legs adds subtle colouring to the otherwise monochrome image. In its compact, dynamic design *Figure (Spanish Woman)* shows Lewis experimenting with his own brand of modernism and anticipates his Vorticist works of 1914–15. LA

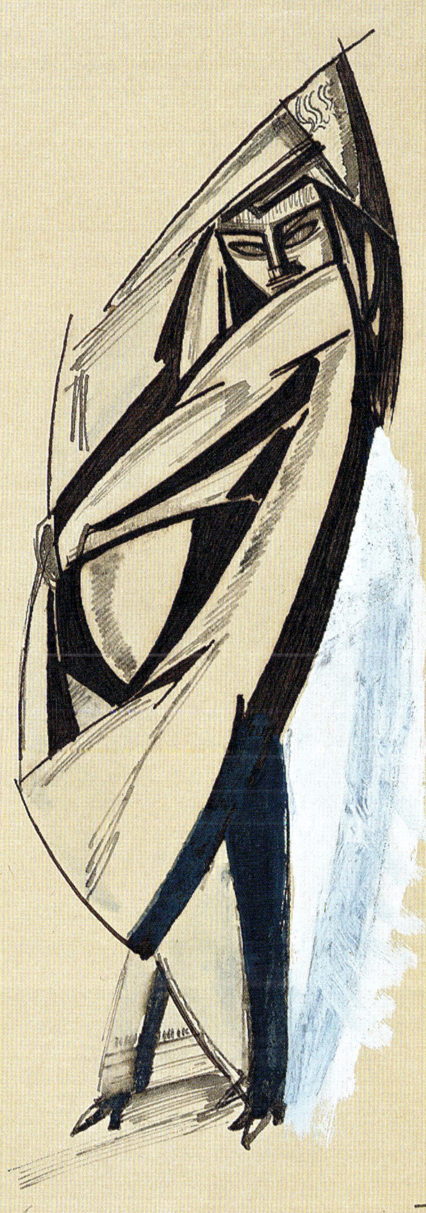
Wyndham Lewis. 1912.

## 6 A MASQUE OF TIMON (*TIMON OF ATHENS*, ACT I) 1912

Pen and ink, watercolour and gouache on paper, 48.5 x 33 [relates to M93]
INSCRIPTIONS 'WL.'
EXHIBITED Second Post-Impressionist Exhibition, Grafton Galleries, London, 1912, no. 211
Wyndham Lewis Memorial Trust: G. and V. Lane collection

Lewis's exposure to continental modernism is clearly evident in this drawing, one of a series executed in the spring or summer of 1912 illustrating Shakespeare's tragedy *Timon of Athens*.[1] In particular, Lewis's dynamic use of arcs and planes attests to his debt to the Futurists, whose work he had seen at an exhibition of their painting at London's Sackville Galleries in March 1912. The *Timon* series represents a crucial moment in the formation of Lewis's own modernist aesthetic, which would lead, two years later, to the 'blastings' and 'blessings' of Vorticism.

The drawing was originally intended for publication within a special edition of the play, although problems with the publisher, Max Goschen, meant that the project was abandoned. Lewis went on to design further drawings for reproduction, publishing a printed portfolio of sixteen *Timon* images, including a version of this drawing, through his fictitious company, The Cube Press, in 1913.

The play concerns the fall of Timon, a man of great wealth whose excessive and foolish generosity leads him to poverty and violent misanthropy. This drawing represents the lavish banquet given by Timon in Scene II, identified by the heraldic trumpet fanfare and the feast which occurs in the receding distance. The dramatic architectural space, in which a succession of candelabra draws the viewer's eye towards this action, creates an arresting backdrop to the moment at which sycophants prey on Timon's naïve goodwill. The masked figure at the centre, raising his goblet in a toast, has been said to be Timon himself, while the figure at the left, holding a staff, may be the character Apemantus observing the scene: 'O you gods, what a number of men eats Timon, and he sees 'em not! It grieves me to see so many dip their meat in one man's blood; and all the madness is, he cheers them up, too. I wonder men dare trust themselves with men.'[2]

While Lewis took on board the visual innovations of Futurism and of Cubist representations of space, the *Timon* series also shows him incorporating philosophical concerns into his work. John Rothenstein, director of the Tate Gallery, described the series as representing 'an attempt to apply Cubism to subjects of wider scope and deeper human concern'.[3] No doubt the subject of the play appealed to Lewis's often antagonistic attitude to the external world.

The drawing is one of a small number of the *Timon* watercolours made for the portfolio still known to be in existence, and was thought for many years to be lost. It was only rediscovered when it appeared for sale at Christie's in 2000, apparently having come from a collection in India. It was then that it was identified as *A Masque of Timon* and acknowledged to be one of six *Timon* drawings exhibited at Roger Fry's Second Post-Impressionist Exhibition. It was from this exhibition in 1912 that the drawing was acquired by the American collector John Quinn. Interestingly, when the drawing next appeared on the market in New York in 1927, it was Lewis who purchased it. He had recently returned to the play in his study *The Lion and the Fox: The Role of the Hero in the Plays of Shakespeare*, published earlier that year. LA

NOTES

1. This lesser-known play is now thought to have been co-written with the dramatist Thomas Middleton. See William Shakespeare and Thomas Middleton, *The Life of Timon of Athens*, ed. John Jowett, Oxford University Press, Oxford, 2004.
2. *Ibid.*, p. 192.
3. John Rothenstein, *Modern English Painters: Lewis to Moore*, Eyre & Spottiswoode, London, 1956, p. 35.

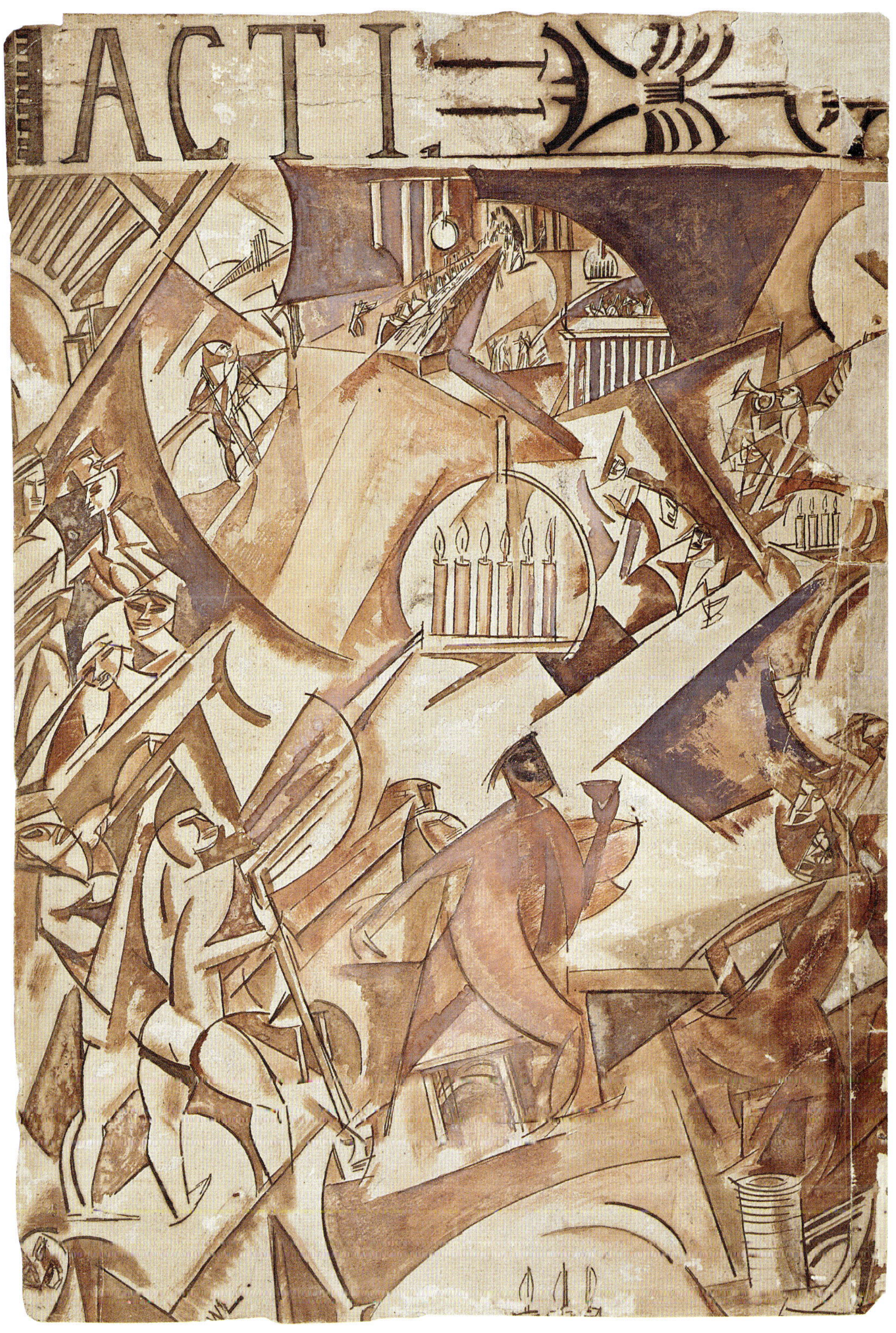
ACT I

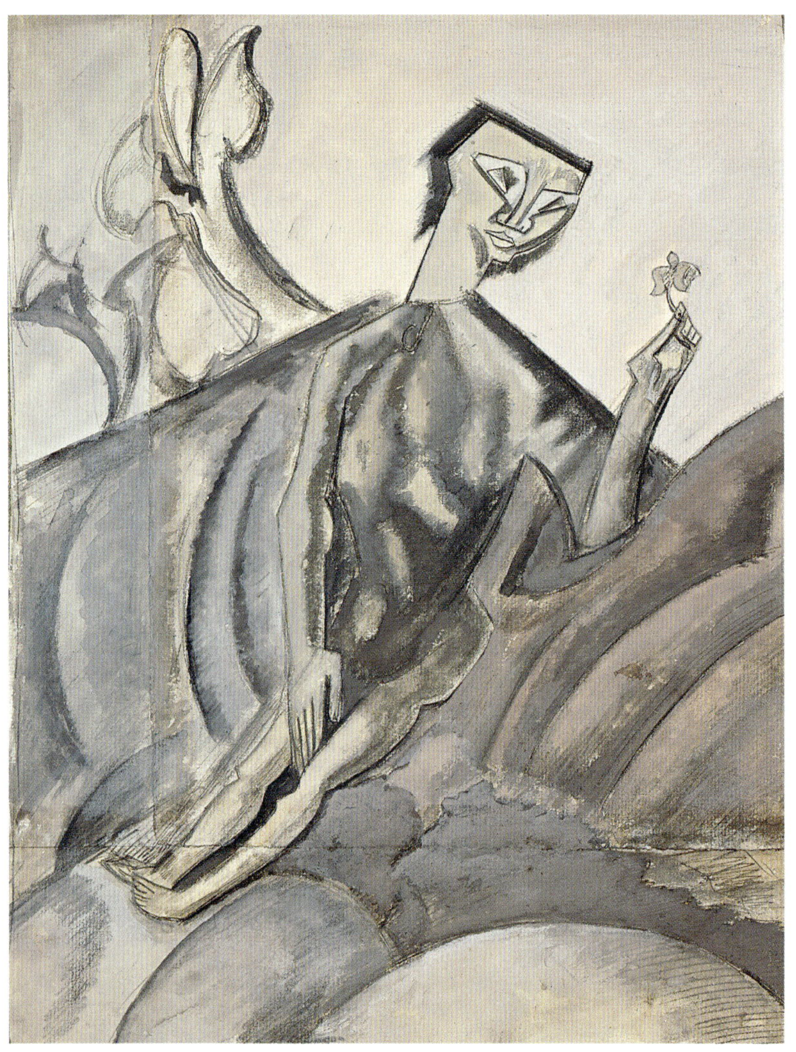

## 7 FIGURE HOLDING A FLOWER 1912

Pencil, pen and ink and gouache on paper, 38.1 x 29.1 [M63]
EXHIBITED *Wyndham Lewis: Drawings and Watercolours 1910–1920*, Anthony d'Offay, London, 1983, no. 8
Walter and Harriet Michel

## 8 FIGURE IN PROFILE 1912

Pencil, pen and ink and gouache on paper, 23.7 x 21.3 [M64]
Walter and Harriet Michel

Lewis's drawings of 1911–12 have a distinctly satirical air. The tragi-comic figures in these two gouache works are the visual embodiment of the satirical characters Lewis wrote about in his 'wild body' stories and essays of 1908–10, pitiable figures of limited intelligence and primitive ways of life. As Lewis later wrote, it was consciousness which he felt marked out civilised man, whereas 'Primitive man has not sorted himself out from nature'.[1] Here, the figures are literally 'at one' with nature, their bodies almost indistinguishable from the rocks and mountains of the barren landscape. In mock-heroic poses one figure gazes skyward, awestruck and confused, while the other stares incomprehensibly at a flower. The satire of the 'wild bodies' was taken to its extreme in drawings like *Two Muscular Figures* (cat. 9) and *Post Jazz* (cat. 10), where the figures' absurd, pumped-up muscles, shrunken heads and nakedness suggest a life governed by physical desires rather than the intellect. JK

NOTE

1. Wyndham Lewis, *Rude Assignment: A Narrative of My Career up-to-date*, Hutchinson, London, 1950, p. 180.

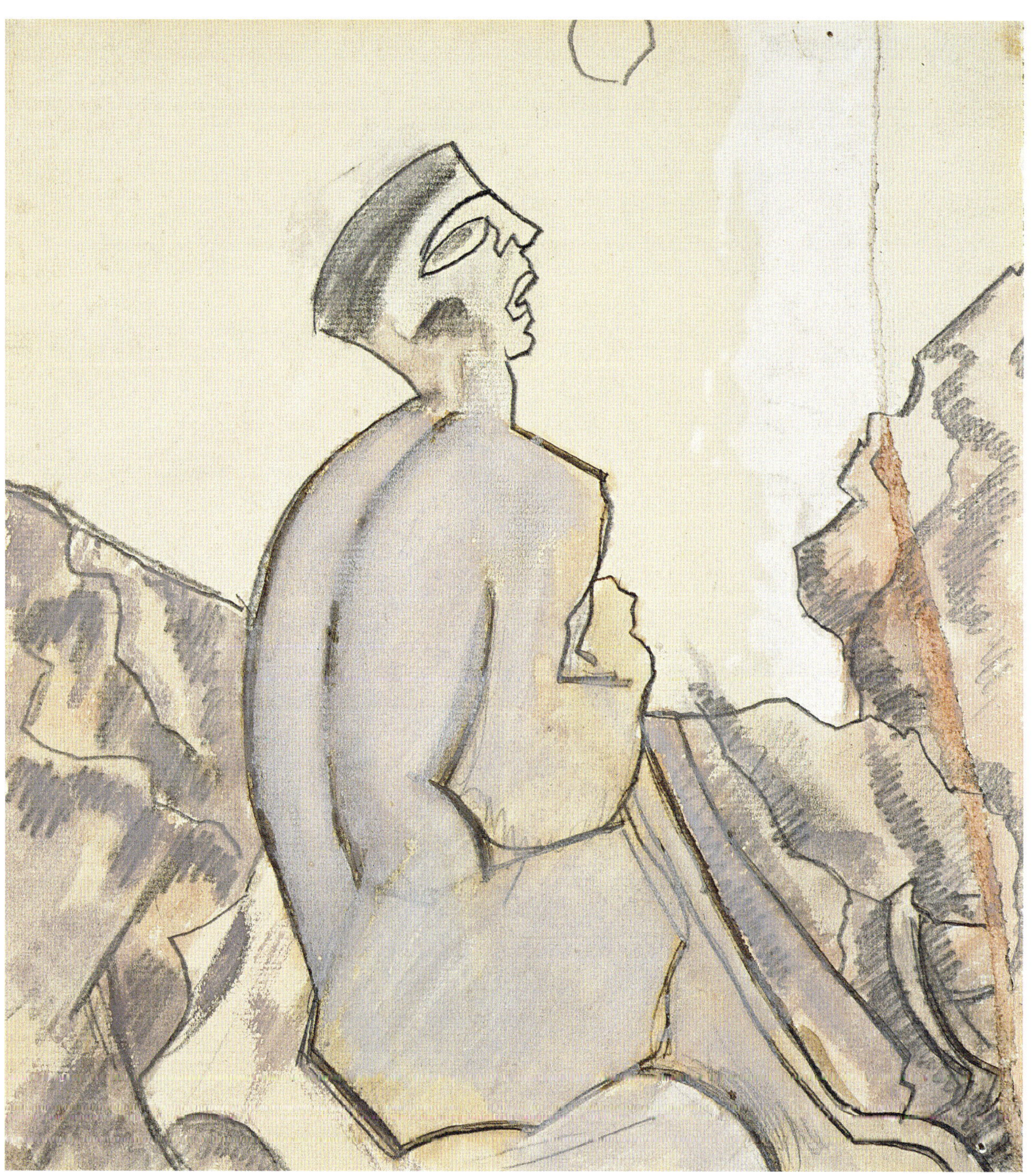

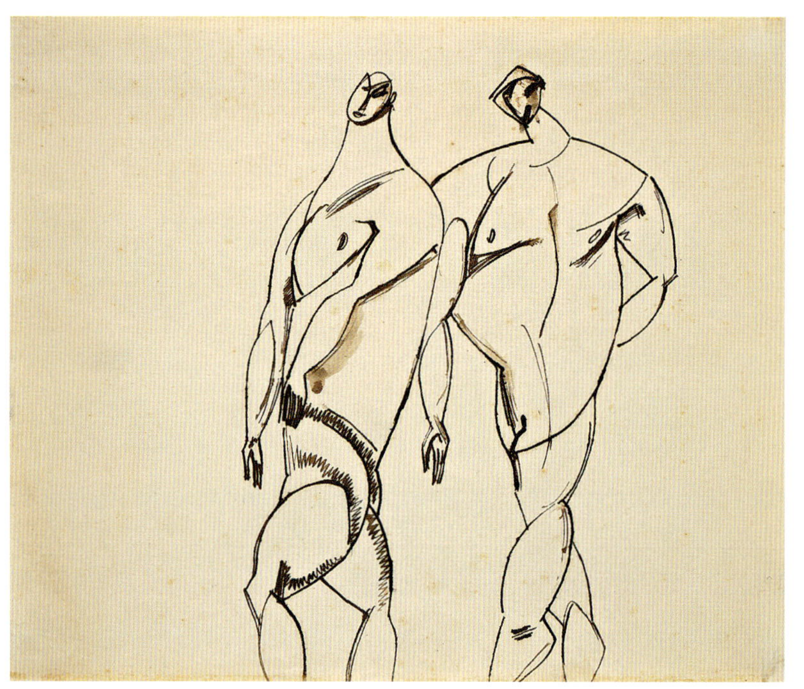

## 9 TWO MUSCULAR FIGURES 1912–13

Pen and ink on paper, 20.2 x 24.3 [M122]
Walter and Harriet Michel

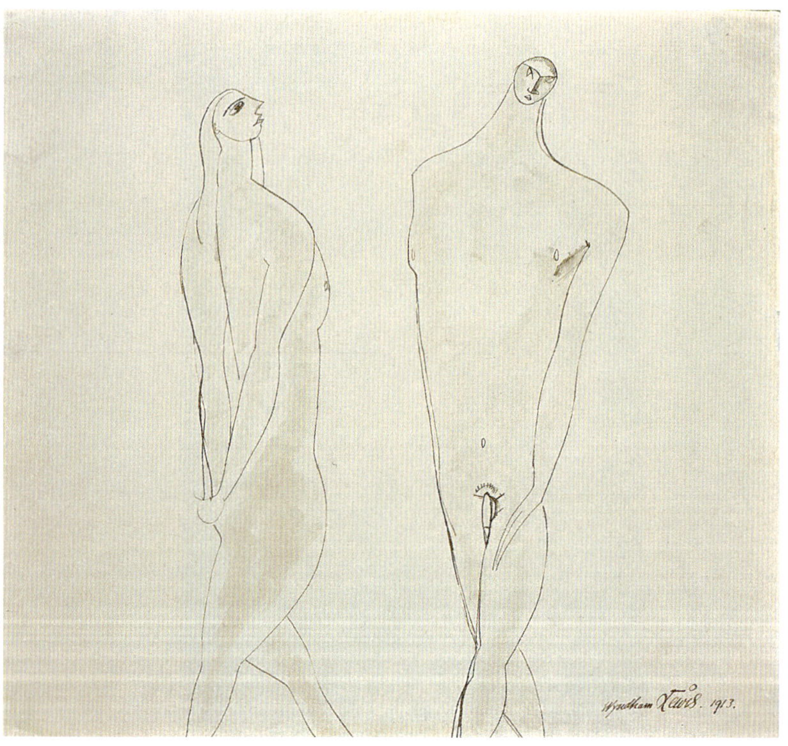


## 10 POST JAZZ 1913

Pen and ink and watercolour on paper, 24.2 x 26.5 [M150]
INSCRIPTIONS 'Wyndham Lewis. 1913.'
EXHIBITED *Paintings and Books by Wyndham Lewis*, York University Art Gallery, Toronto, 1964, no. 55
Private collection

## 11 **NIJINSKI 1914**

Pen and ink and ink wash on paper,
19.9 × 22.5 [M168]
INSCRIPTIONS 'W.L. 1914.' and
'Nijinski.'
Private collection

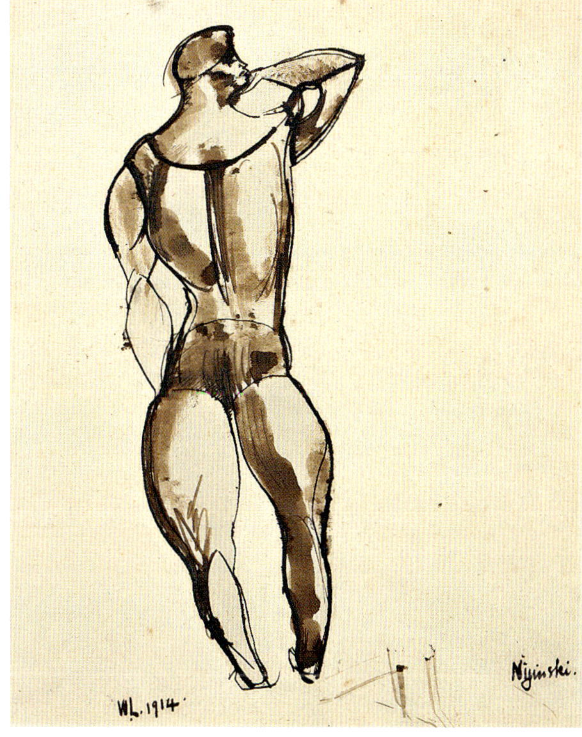


## 12 **NIJINSKI 1914**

Pen and ink and ink wash on paper,
20.2 × 22.8 [M169]
Private collection

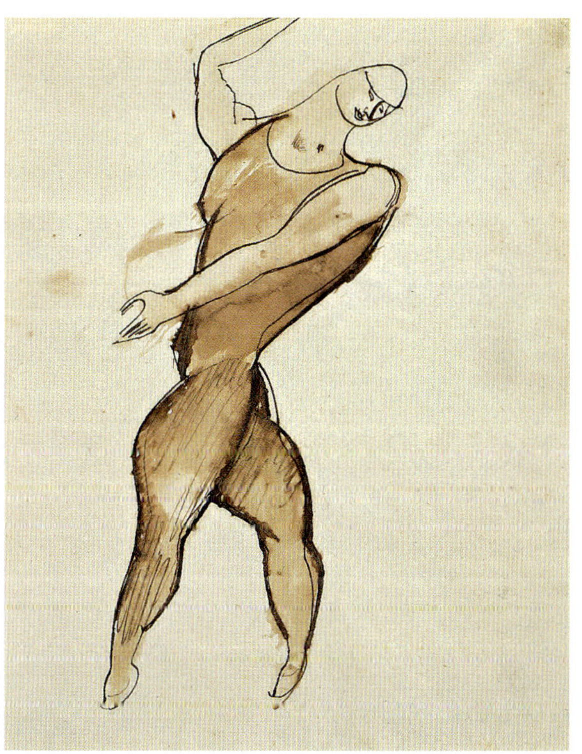

## 13 **DRAGON IN A CAGE 1914–15 (completed 1950)**

Pen and ink, chalk and gouache on paper, 47.7 x 34.8 [M164]
INSCRIPTIONS 'Wyndham Lewis 1950'
EXHIBITED *Wyndham Lewis*, Santa Barbara Museum of Art, Santa Barbara, 1957, no. 4; *Wyndham Lewis: Drawings and Watercolours 1910–1920*, Anthony d'Offay, London, 1983, no. 23
Private collection

By 1914 Lewis had established the Vorticist movement, together with the writer Ezra Pound and a number of artists including Edward Wadsworth and Henri Gaudier-Brzeska. Initially a rebellion against what was viewed as the stifling world of the Bloomsbury Group, Vorticism was also a reaction to artistic trends further afield, and absorbed forms of visual expression found in Cubism and Futurism. However, the group developed a theoretical position which separated their art from these movements, and they announced their alternative manifesto in the journal *Blast*, produced in two issues in June 1914 and July 1915.

The Vorticists sought to capture the vigour of urban life and Lewis's Vorticist style was epitomised by often vertiginous geometric designs which mimicked the architectural order of the modern metropolis. *Dragon in a Cage* began life as one of these Vorticist compositions in around 1914–15. Lewis reworked the drawing some 35 years later, transforming its geometry into a fantastical landscape. At the upper left, planetary forms are introduced, similar to those found in the cosmic imagery of works such as *Creation Myth* (cat. 49). At the right, the dragon is constructed from the abstract elements of the original design, a linear arrangement which appears simultaneously to form the dragon's ribcage and the bars which keep the animal captive. The image of the dragon is completed with smoke bellowing from its mouth, and a curving tail. Despite these alterations, the dynamic configurations of the Vorticist work remain fixed, particularly the central, jutting armature which holds the composition together. The strict Vorticist framework is further emphasised by the underlying grid squared-off by the artist, still visible in unmarked areas. The accents of colour, particularly the electric blue, are typical of Lewis's vibrant palette.

That Lewis introduced elements of representation into a previously abstract composition in 1950 is curious. However, in 1954, he was openly to reject his former foray into abstraction in his book *The Demon of Progress in the Arts*, in which he characterised 'extremism' in art as a 'disease': 'The first case to be reported in these islands was mine, around 1913 .... Fortunately, with me the disease did not have time to mature. Another scourge, namely war, intervened .... So of course I recovered my reason. I escaped ... from reaching that point, very soon, where I should have ceased to be a *visual* artist at all. For what I was headed for, obviously, was to fly away from the world of men, of pigs, of chickens and alligators, and to go to live in the unwatered moon, only a moon sawed up into square blocks, in the most alarming way. What an escape I had!'[1]

*Dragon in a Cage* testifies to Lewis's complex and highly imaginative mind, drawing together not only the beginning and end of his career but also two extremes of his visual oeuvre – the dynamic structures of Vorticism and the playful, often surreal imagery of his later years. LA

NOTE

1. Wyndham Lewis, *The Demon of Progress in the Arts* (1954), Methuen, London, 1955, p. 3.

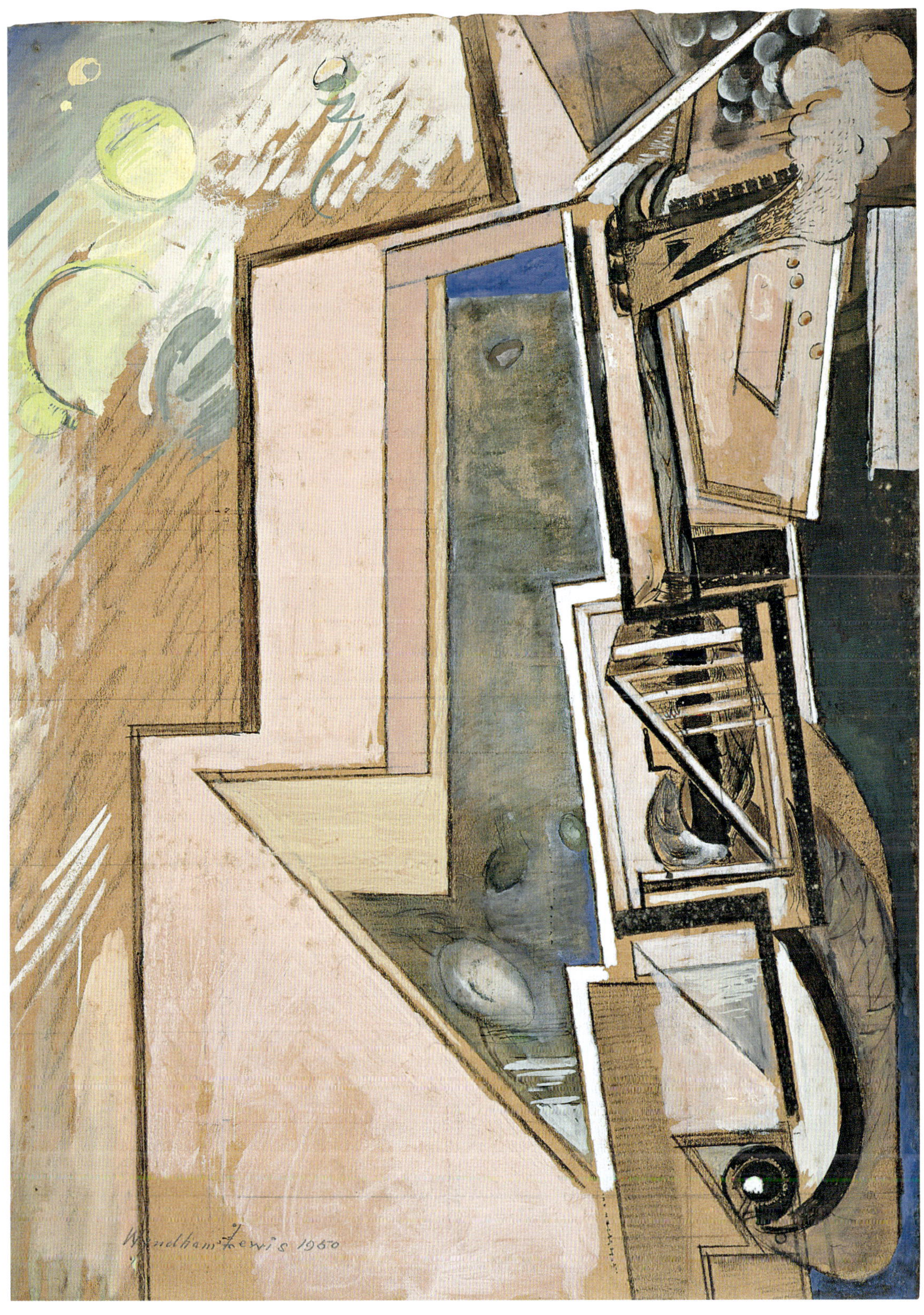
Wyndham Lewis 1950

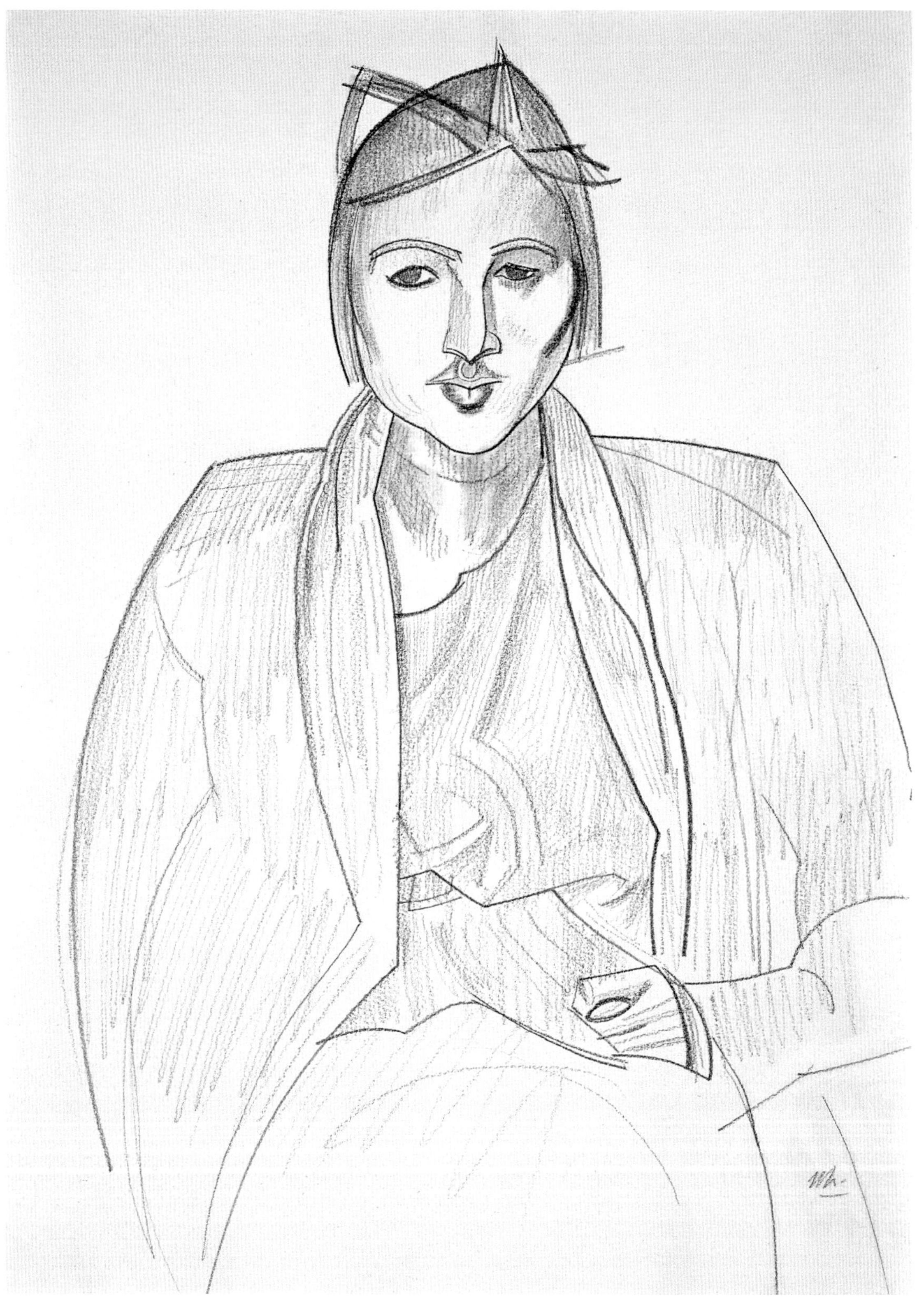

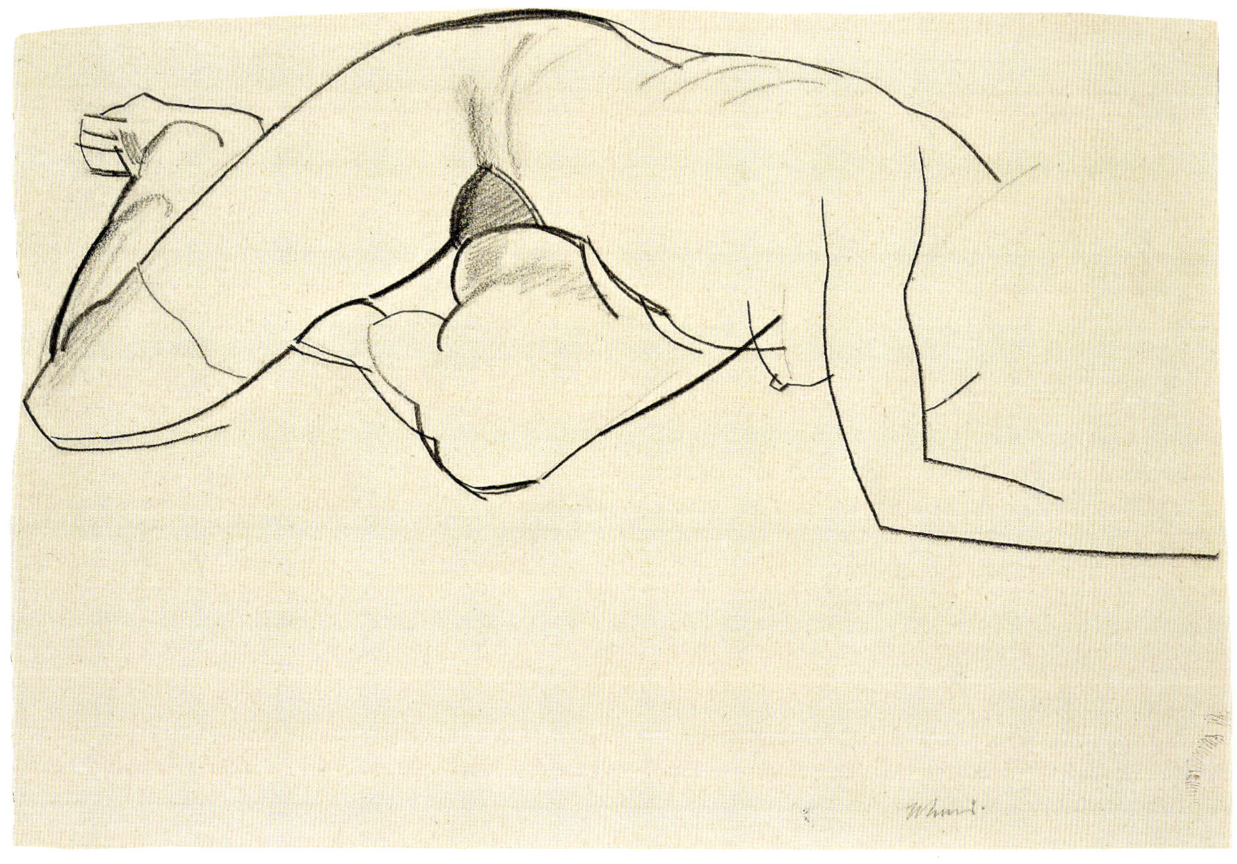

## 14 **LADY WITH HAT 1919**

Chalk on paper, 35.5 × 25.5 [M335]
INSCRIPTIONS 'WL.'
EXHIBITED *Wyndham Lewis: Drawings and Watercolours 1910–1920*, Anthony d'Offay, London, 1983, no. 38
Private collection

## 15 **RECLINING NUDE 1919–20**

Chalk on paper, 22.9 × 32 [M374]
INSCRIPTIONS 'W Lewis.'
Walter and Harriet Michel

Following his experiences during the First World War, Lewis's art underwent a significant change. He abandoned the abstract compositions of Vorticism and, instead, confronted 'the flesh and blood' of life.[1] Lewis became preoccupied with the human body, making numerous pencil and chalk drawings of striking clarity, such as *Lady with Hat* (left). His studies of female nudes are particularly arresting for their unusual compositional arrangements. *Reclining Nude* is exemplary of this return to the figure and displays Lewis's ability to create form through a succession of taut chalk lines. IA

NOTE

1. Wyndham Lewis, *Rude Assignment: A Narrative of My Career up-to-date*, Hutchinson, London, 1950, p. 129.

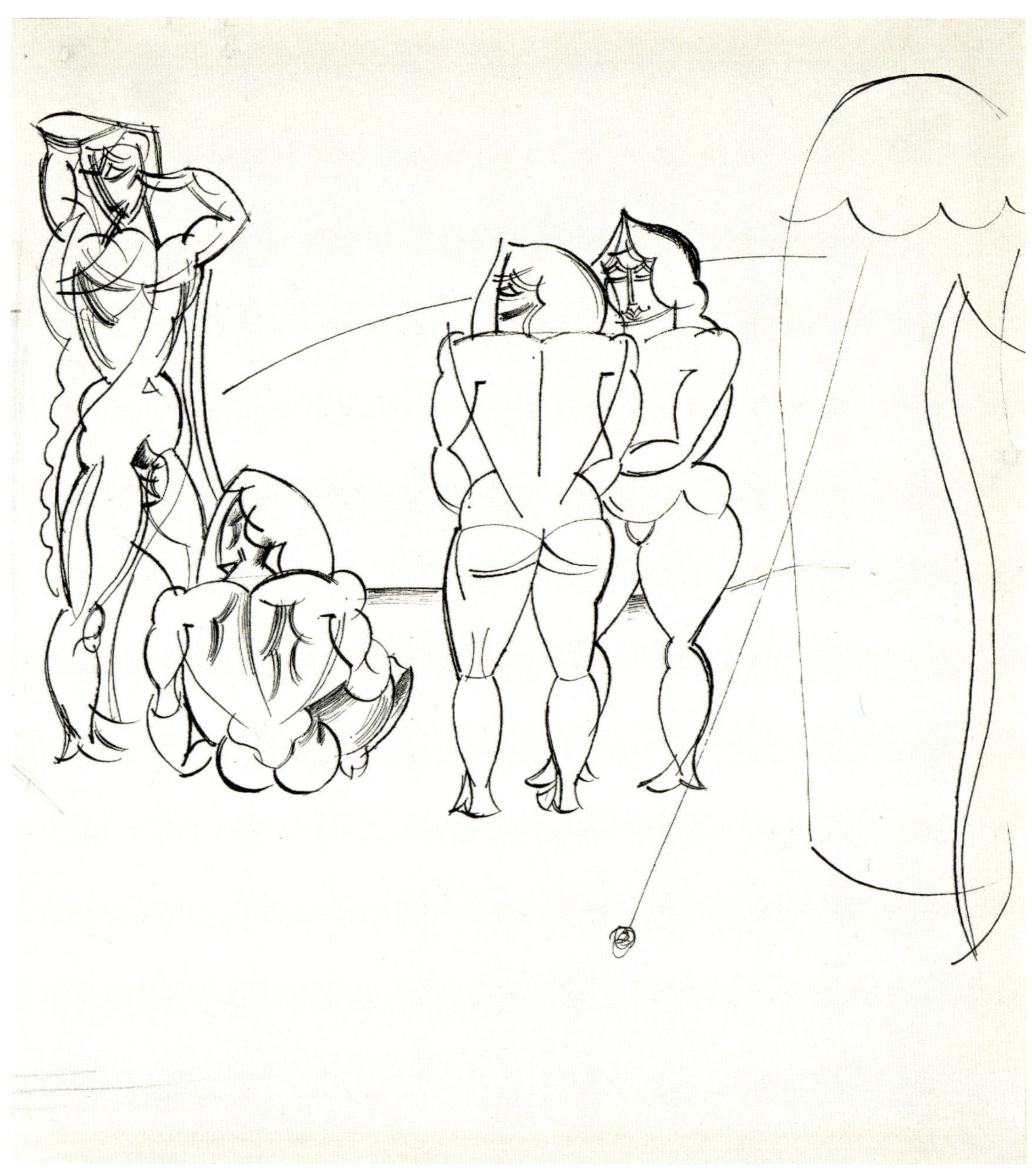

16 **FIGURES AT A BEACH HOUSE 1919–20**

Pen and ink and pencil on paper,
30.1 x 27.1 [M368]
Private collection

## 17 **BATHERS 1919–20**

Pen and ink, watercolour and gouache on paper, 38.2 x 25.1 [M363]
Private collection

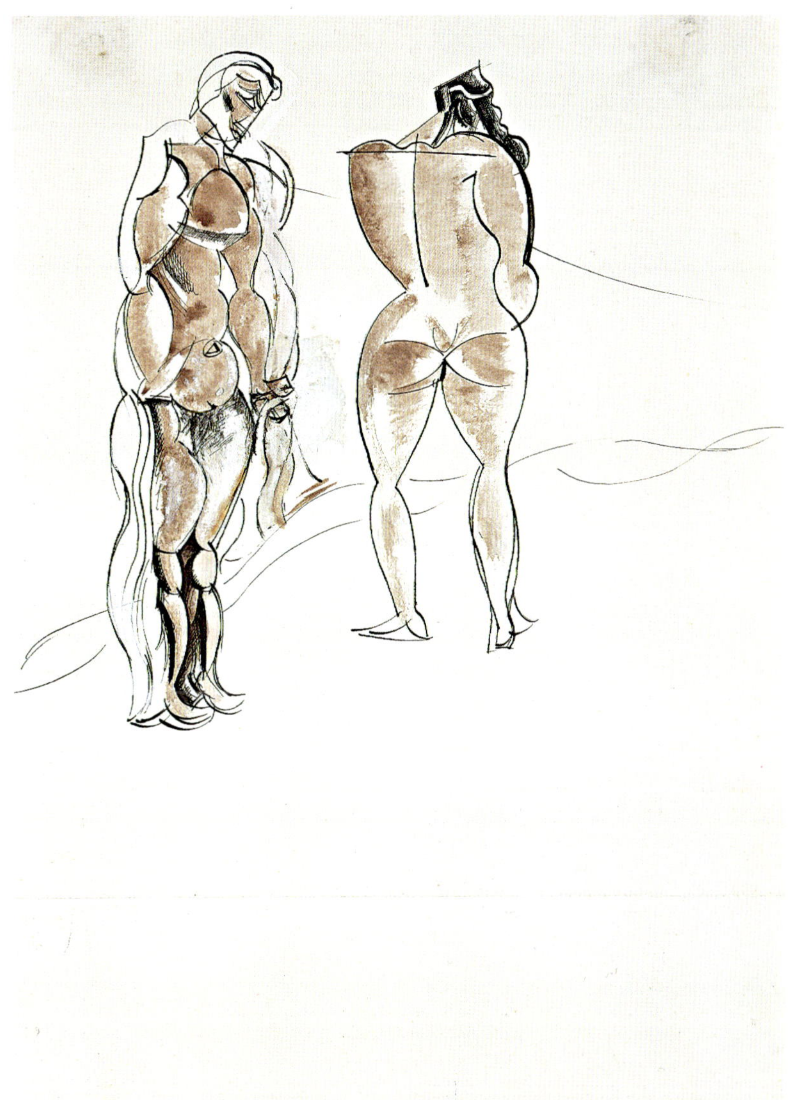

Bathing was a popular theme among many modernist artists, and became a recurrent motif in Lewis's work from the 1910s to the 1930s (see, for example, cat. 43). While the German Expressionists had stressed the sensuality and freedom of the open air and the invigorating lack of social restraints which bathing offered, Lewis adapted the motif in a critique of both modern social mores and the modernist tradition itself. In *Figures at a Beach House* the beach hut becomes a redundant symbol of propriety as the bathers flagrantly, and grotesquely, parade themselves by the shore, gawping at one another's nudity. In *Bathers*, Lewis satirises sex and gender, the hermaphrodite figure at the left parodying the usual stereotype of male desire. In both drawings the subject-matter and angular treatment of the figures seem to be a direct critique of the 'primitivism' so much in vogue among avant-garde artists like Picasso and Derain, whose work Lewis knew from his regular trips to Paris. JK

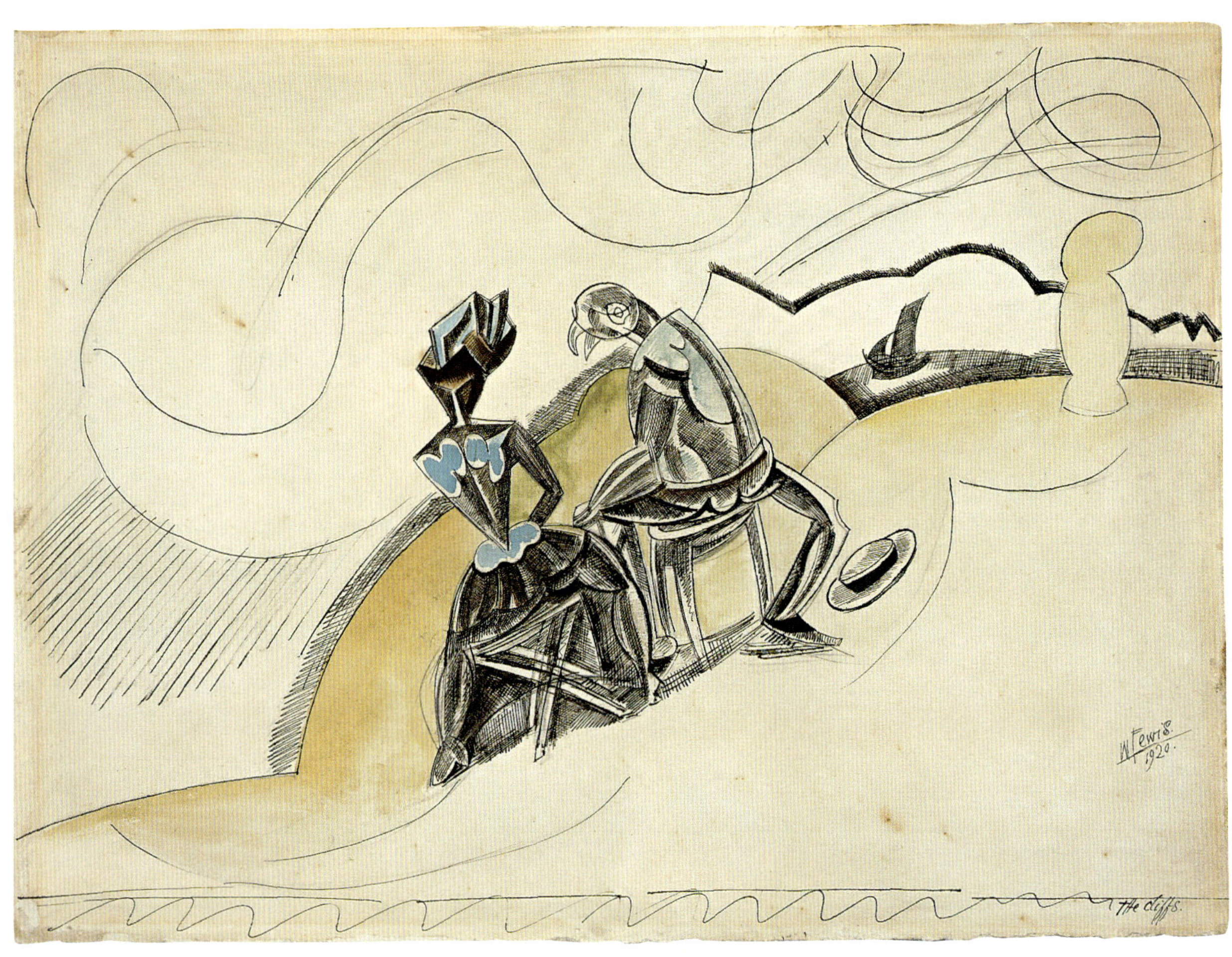


18 **THE CLIFFS 1920**

Pencil, pen and ink, watercolour and gouache on paper, 28.2 × 37.9 [M388]
INSCRIPTIONS 'W Lewis 1920.' and 'The cliffs.'
Wyndham Lewis Memorial Trust: G. and V. Lane collection

19 **SEATED LADY 1921**

Pencil on paper, 44.4 × 30.6 [M478]
Private collection

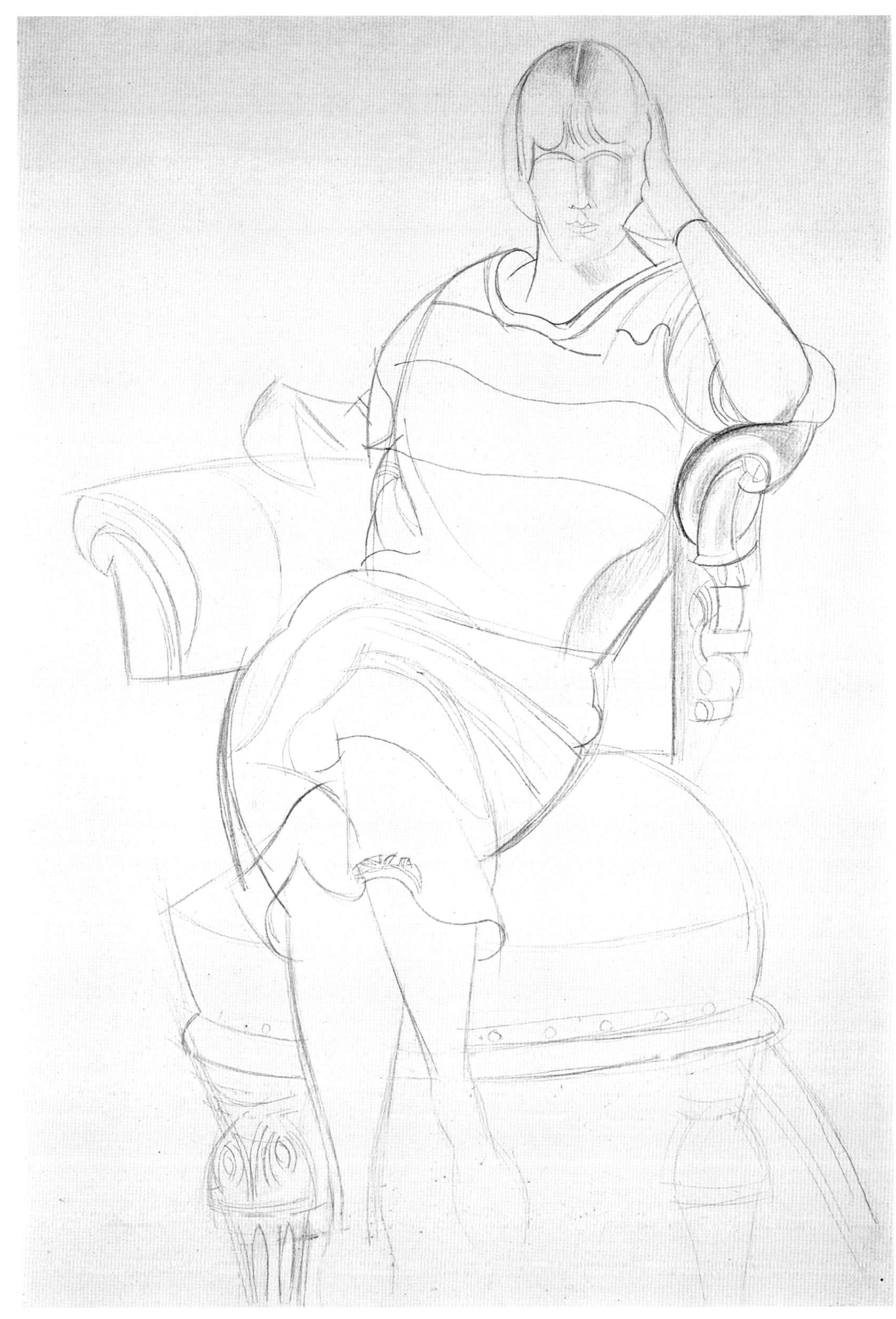

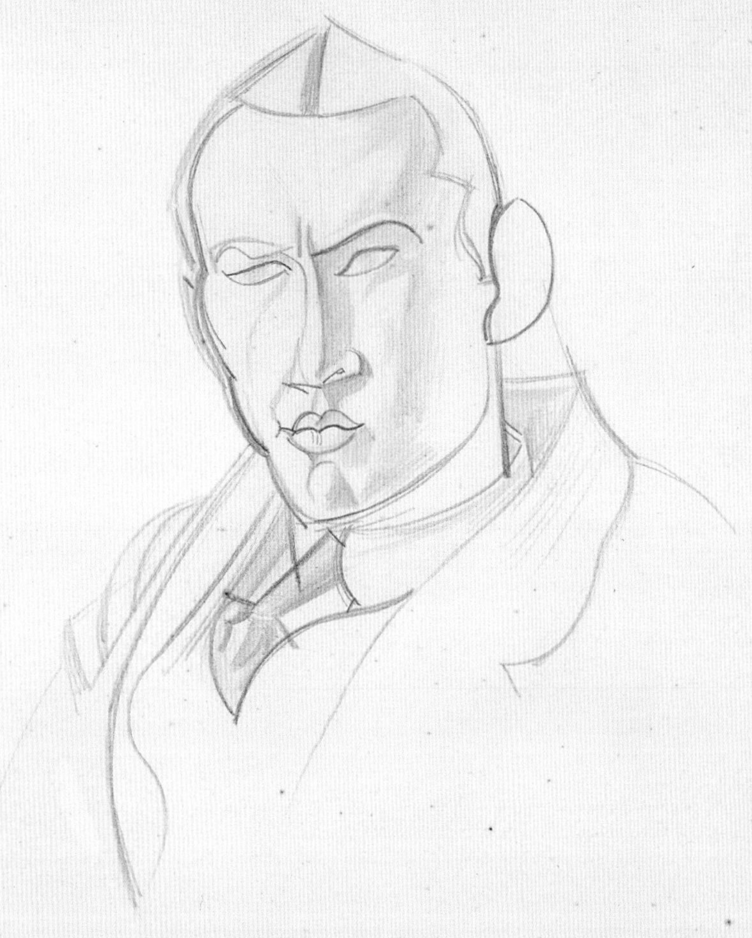
Wyndham Lewis. 1921. (June.)
B. ROWLAND.

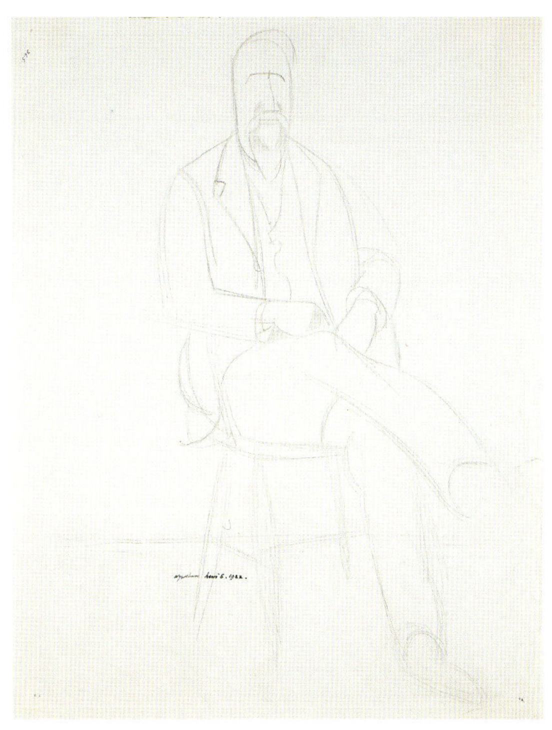

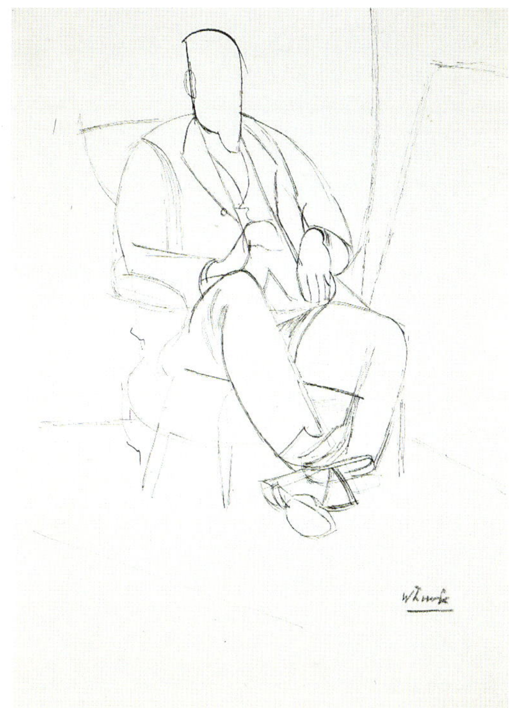

*left*

20 **PORTRAIT OF BERNARD ROWLAND 1921**

Pencil on paper, 36.2 × 25.6

INSCRIPTIONS 'B. Rowland.' and 'Wyndham Lewis. 1921. (June.)'

Wyndham Lewis Memorial Trust: G. and V. Lane collection

*above left*

21 **STUDY FOR PAINTING OF EDWIN EVANS 1922**

Pencil on paper, 37.8 × 29 [M530]

INSCRIPTIONS 'Wyndham Lewis. 1922.'; *verso*: 'for oil of Evans (music critic)'

Private collection

*above right*

22 **STUDY FOR PAINTING OF EDWIN EVANS 1922**

Pen and ink on paper, 36.7 × 25.9 [M529]

INSCRIPTIONS 'W Lewis'; *verso*: 'for oil of Evans. (music critic)'

Private collection

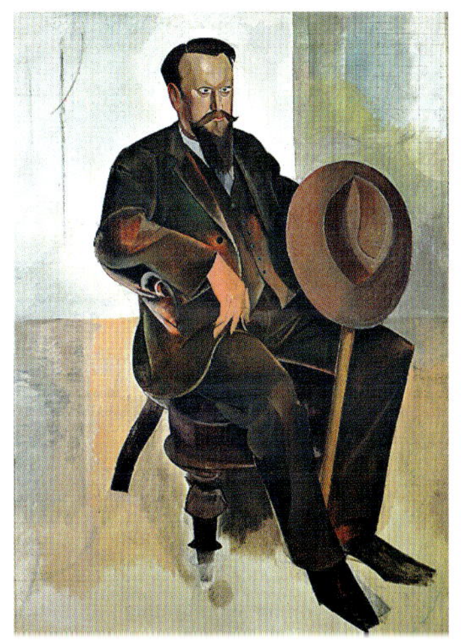

*Portrait of Edwin Evans*, 1922, oil on canvas, 150 × 108 [M P35]
Scottish National Gallery of Modern Art, Edinburgh

In 1922 Lewis was commissioned to paint Edwin Evans, an important music critic, to honour Evans's active role in promoting modern music in Britain.

## 23 **WOMEN 1921–22**

Pen and ink, ink wash and gouache on paper, 27.5 x 21.3 [M518]
Wyndham Lewis Memorial Trust:
G. and V. Lane collection

By the early 1920s Lewis was working in a variety of visual styles, from taut line drawings (cat. 15) to more deliberately experimental works such as this. In common with numerous drawings of the period, in *Women* he combined figurative and abstract elements into the design, creating strange, totem-like figures built up from a complex amalgam of forms. More sculptural than human, the three characters stand rigidly on what seems to be a stage, the white paper suggesting the bright glow of the footlights and a curtain hanging at the right. Borrowing from the language of synthetic Cubism, Lewis employed a collage effect to render the material surface of his figures, the mock wood-grain of the woman in profile at the left adding to the figure's sculptural presence.

Lewis's depiction of the three women shows the influence of non-Western art, which he had long admired. Writing to the American art critic and collector James Thrall Soby in 1947, Lewis noted how, in his own work, 'Polynesian influences ... occur all along. We have here in the British Museum some very fine collections of New Ireland masks, Easter Island monoliths, and other varieties of Pacific and S. America [*sic*] stuff. Even when at the Slade School I was directed to go to the Print Room at the Museum and study the drawings of Raphael and Michelangelo I had always to pass between cases full of more savage symbols on my way to the shrines of the cinquecento ....'[1] Soby reproduced this drawing the following year in his book on contemporary painters, citing the references it made to Oceanic sculpture.

While Lewis came to criticise what he saw as an over-dependence on 'primitivism' by contemporary artists such as Amedeo Modigliani, his palpable rejection of Western canons of beauty in works like *Women* was of great significance to his artistic credo. In these drawings he attempted to convey, in visual form, a critique of the art of antiquity and of the Renaissance, as well as of the modern-day fashion, evident in Paris especially, for a return to classical models of art. In his 1919 book *The Caliph's Design: Architects! Where is your Vortex?*, he attacked the 'return to order' and the zealous craze, sweeping the contemporary art world, for neo-classicism. His aversion to French aesthetic fashions may have encouraged him to decline an offer, made by the art dealer Léonce Rosenberg in 1922, to exhibit some of his pictures at the Galerie L'Effort Moderne in Paris. In an article entitled 'Paris versus the World' of the previous year, he had attempted to show how it was far from necessary to work in the French capital in order to be a cutting-edge artist: '... the only thing really to consider is whether the European artist to-day had better pitch his tent in Paris, or whether he might equally well elect to live in Bohemia, Lancashire, or Andalusia. He can, in almost any part of Europe, acquaint himself from day to day with the phases of thought and developments of fashion occurring in other parts of Europe, if he wish'.[2]

In his experimental drawings of 1921–22 Lewis consciously sought to create an aesthetic which would provide the momentum for a new post-war avant-garde art. When *Women* was reproduced in 1922 in the second edition of Lewis's satirical journal *The Tyro*, he announced in the editorial that 'The painting, sculpture and general design of to-day, such as can be included in the movement we support, aims at nothing short of a physical reconstruction and reordering of the visible part of our world'.[3] JK

NOTES

1 Letter to James Thrall Soby, 9 April 1947, in *The Letters of Wyndham Lewis*, ed. W.K. Rose, Methuen, London, 1963, p. 407.

2 Wyndham Lewis, 'Paris versus the world', *The Dial*, vol. 71, no. 1, July 1921, p. 25.

3 Wyndham Lewis, *The Tyro: A Review of the Arts of Painting, Sculpture and Design*, no. 2 (1922), Frank Cass, London, 1970, p. 5.

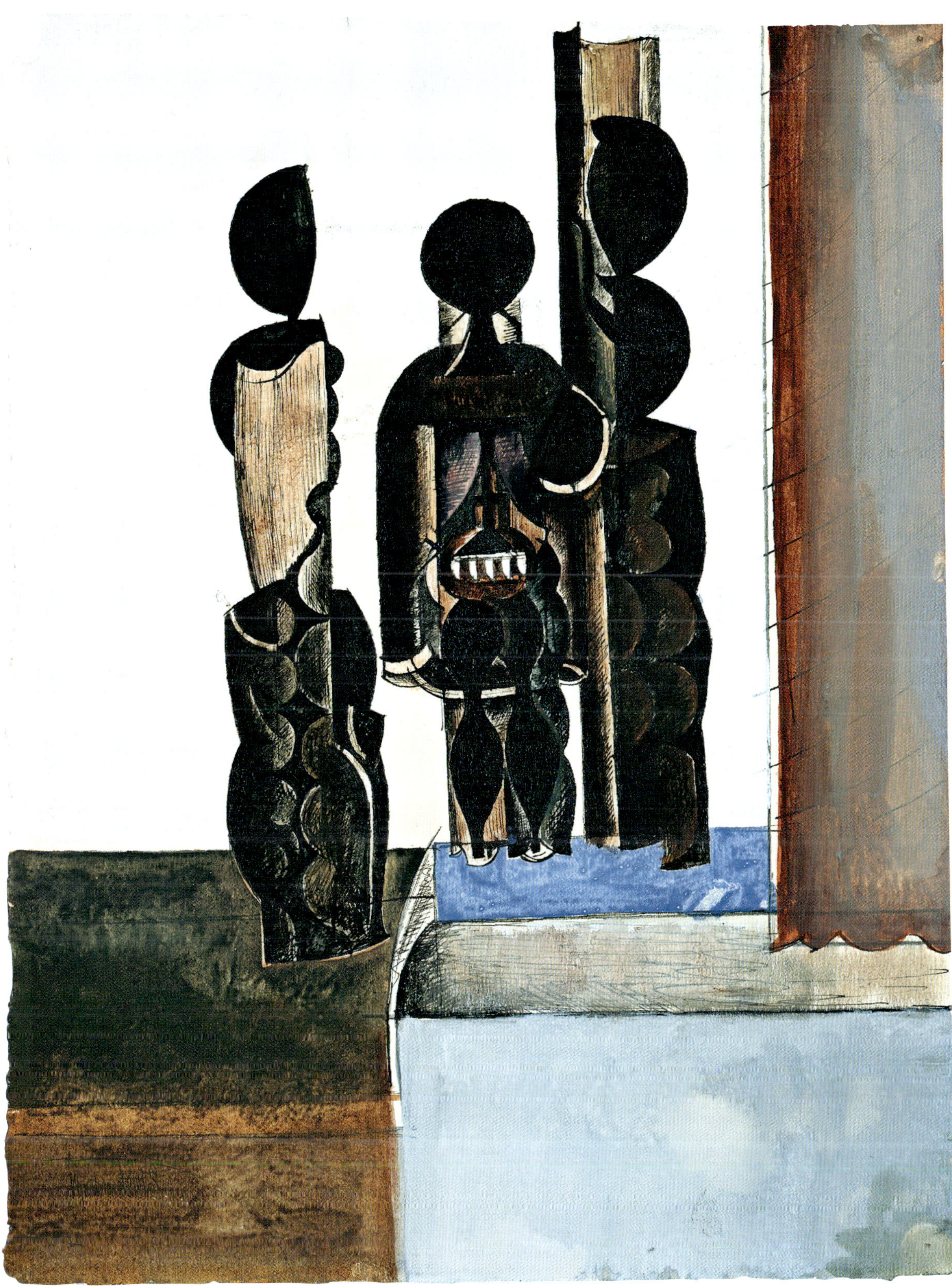

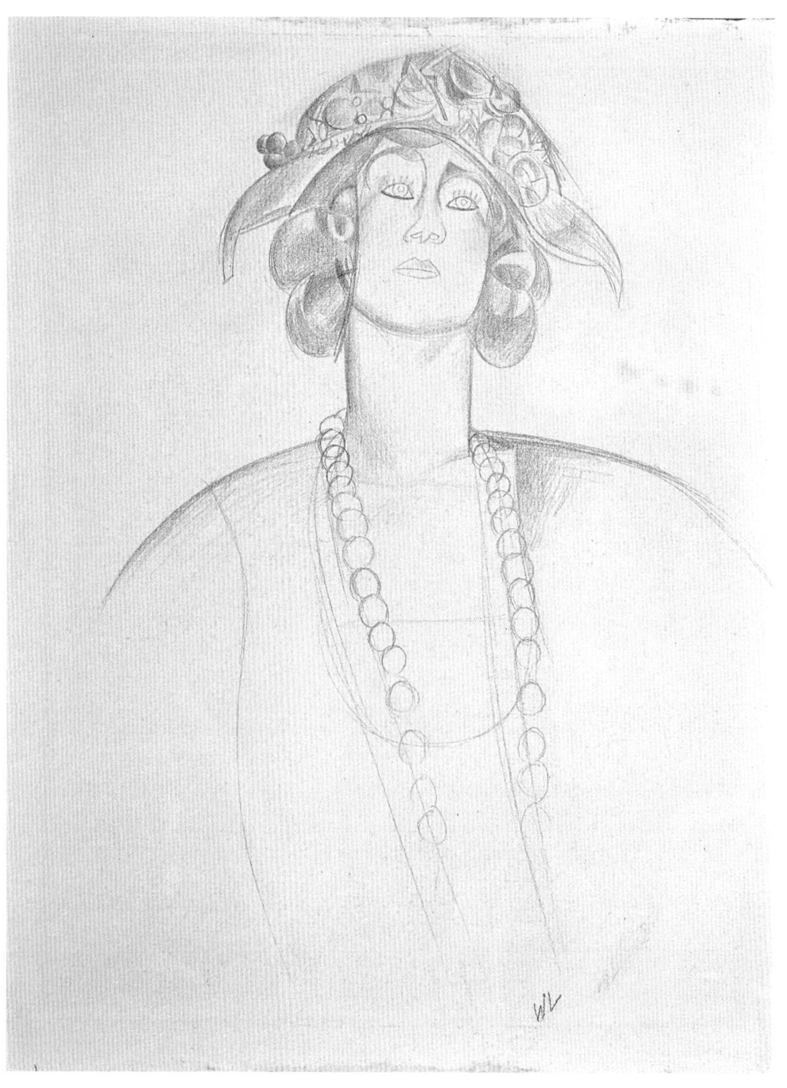


## 24 **VIOLET TSCHIFFELY Early 1920s**

Pencil on paper, 31 × 22.8
INSCRIPTIONS 'WL' with another inscription erased
Wyndham Lewis Memorial Trust: Porteus gift

## 25 **THREE SISTERS 1927**

Pen and ink and gouache on paper, 38.5 × 28.5 [M643]
INSCRIPTIONS 'Wyndham Lewis. October 1927.'
Wyndham Lewis Memorial Trust: G. and V. Lane collection

The decorative stylisation of *Three Sisters*, with its figures set against a bare ground, strong colours blocked out over black ink, and the fluid compositional relationship between the three women, shares many of the distinctive qualities of Japanese *ukiyo-e* woodblock prints. Lewis may well have been aware of these through his acquaintance with Laurence Binyon, curator of prints and drawings at the British Museum, who had written extensively on Eastern art and aesthetics. *Three Sisters* was made during a period of intense literary production for Lewis and is a rare example of the visual art he was making at this time. When he reproduced the work in the journal *Drawing and Design* in 1929 to accompany his essay 'A World Art and Tradition', the work was entitled *Three Figures*. He described how such a drawing might seem 'to the casual commercial eye of the same order as the first Chinese or Japanese work seen in Europe; as first and foremost a curiosity'. LA

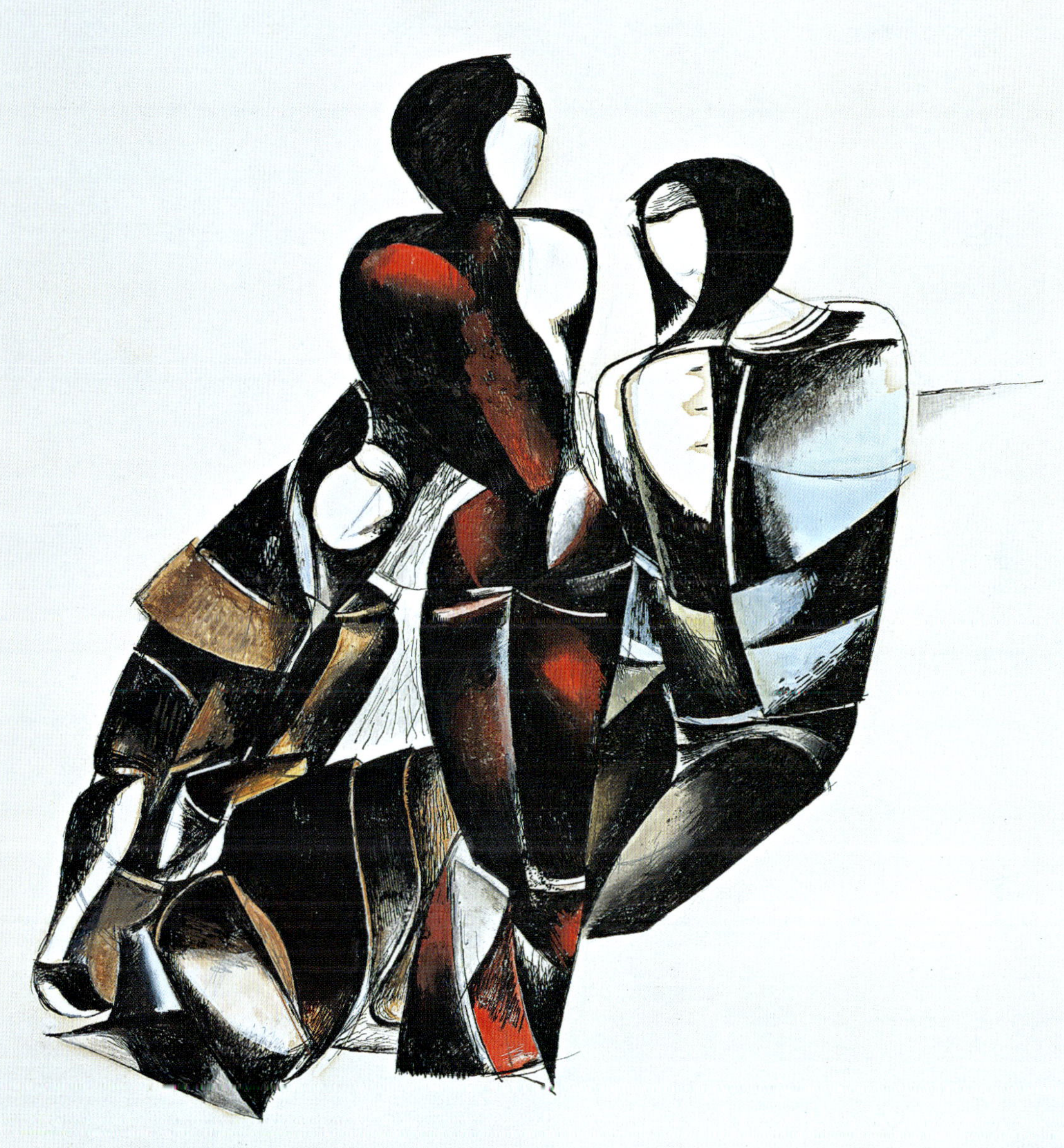
WYNDHAM LEWIS. OCtoBER 1927.

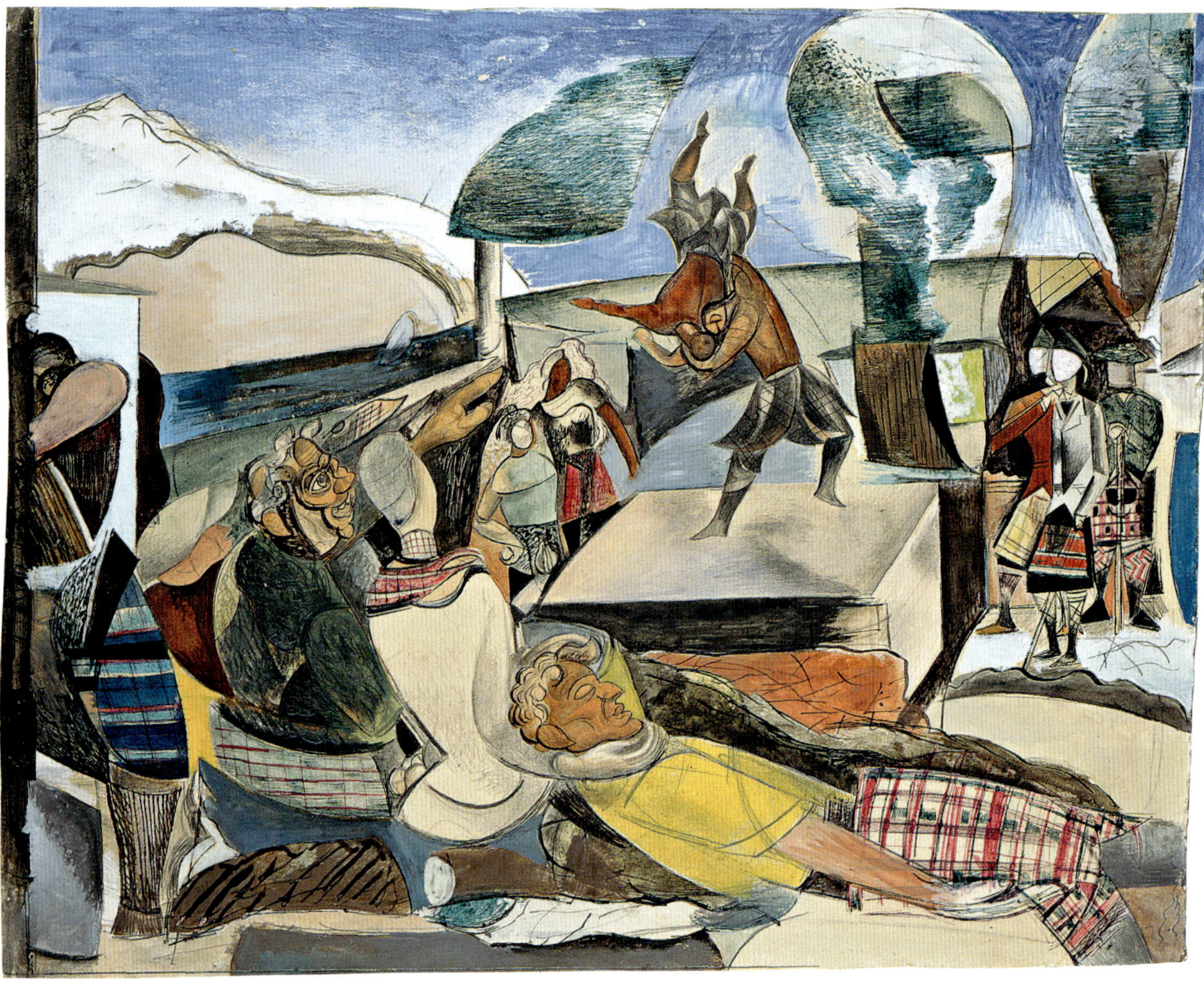

*above*
### 26 **WRESTLING 1929**

Pencil, pen and ink, watercolour and gouache on paper, 34.5 x 43.1 [M654]
EXHIBITED *Wyndham Lewis: The Twenties*, Anthony d'Offay, London, 1984, no. 34
Walter and Harriet Michel

*right above*
### 27 **BERBER BOY 1931**

Pencil and watercolour on card, 36.9 x 25.1 [M709]
INSCRIPTION 'Wyndham Lewis 1931.'
EXHIBITED *Paintings and Drawings by Wyndham Lewis*, Leicester Galleries, London, 1937, no. 26
Wyndham Lewis Memorial Trust: G. and V. Lane collection

*right below*
### 28 **DESERT SOUK 1931**

Pencil, watercolour and gouache on paper, 22.1 x 35.2 [M711]
INSCRIPTIONS 'Wyndham Lewis. 1931.'; *verso*: 'Desert Souk'
EXHIBITED *French and English Contemporary Artists*, Zwemmer Gallery, London 1934, no. 36
Wyndham Lewis Memorial Trust: Fox collection

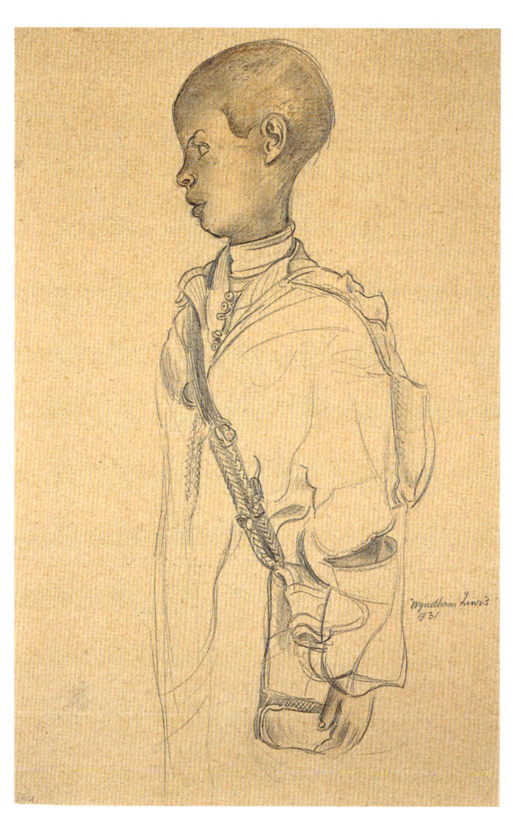


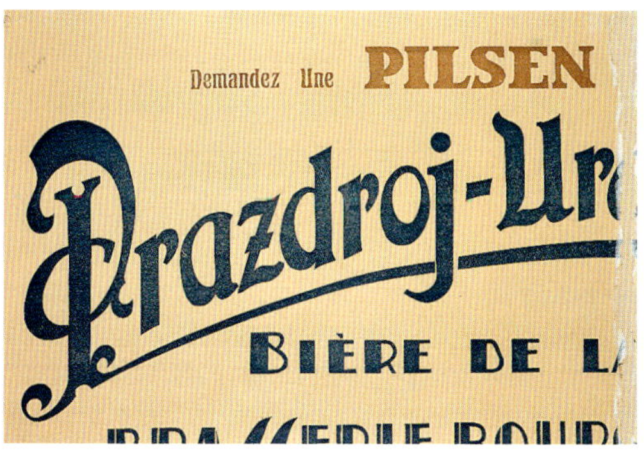


Verso of cat. 27

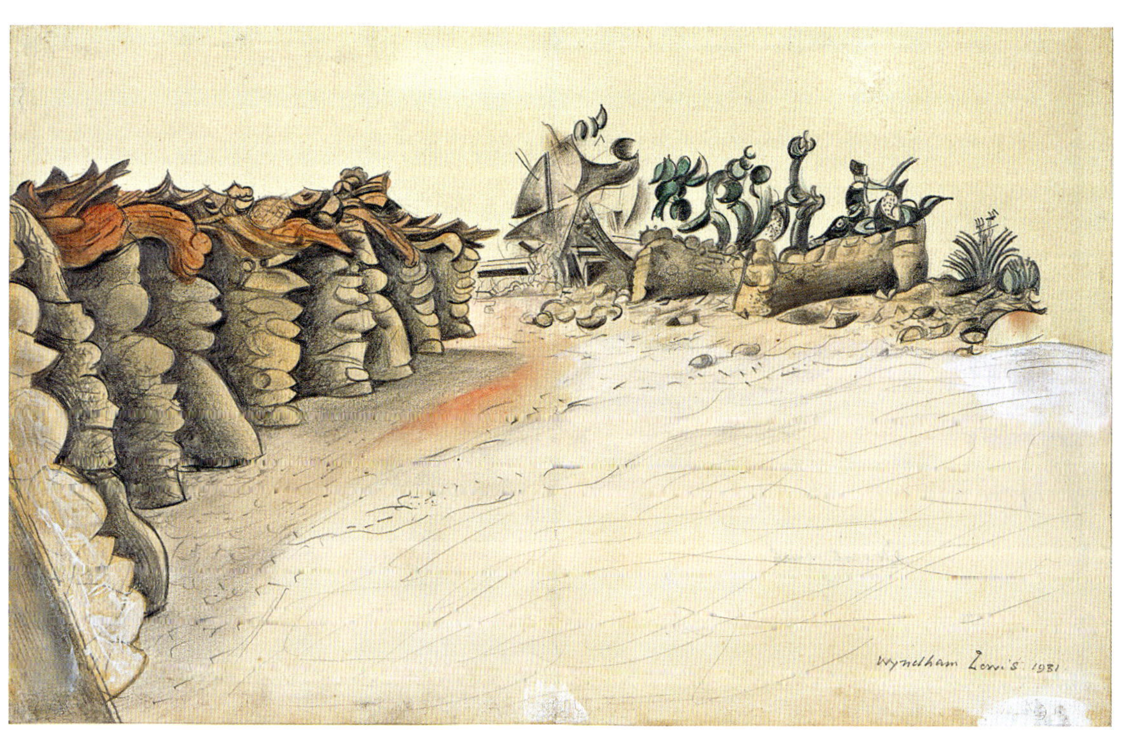

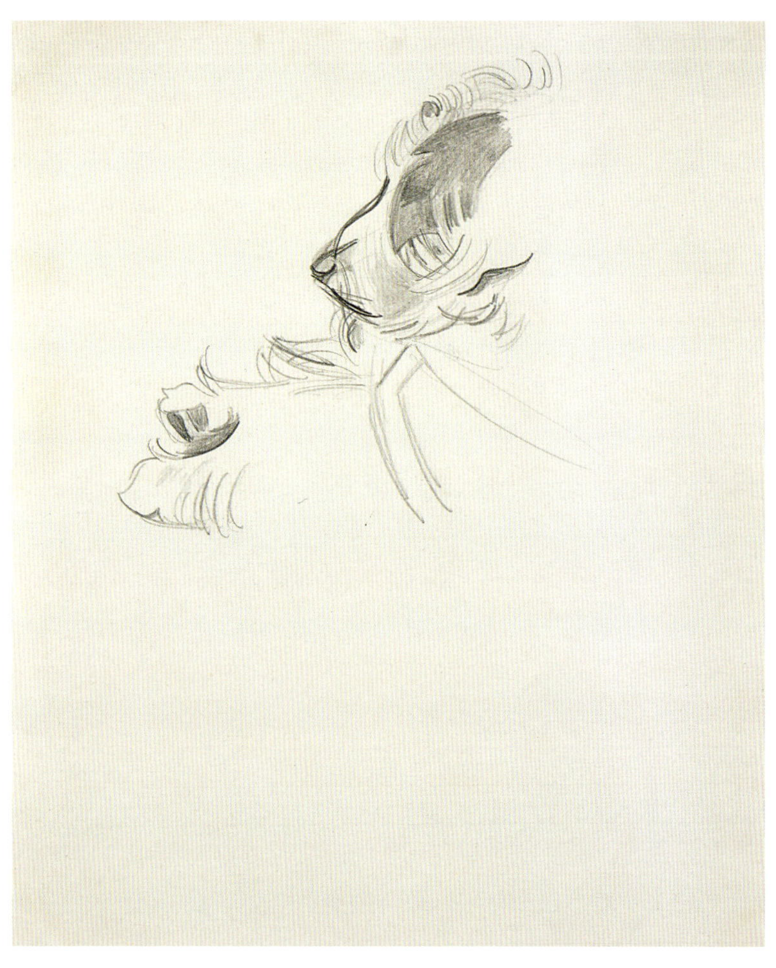

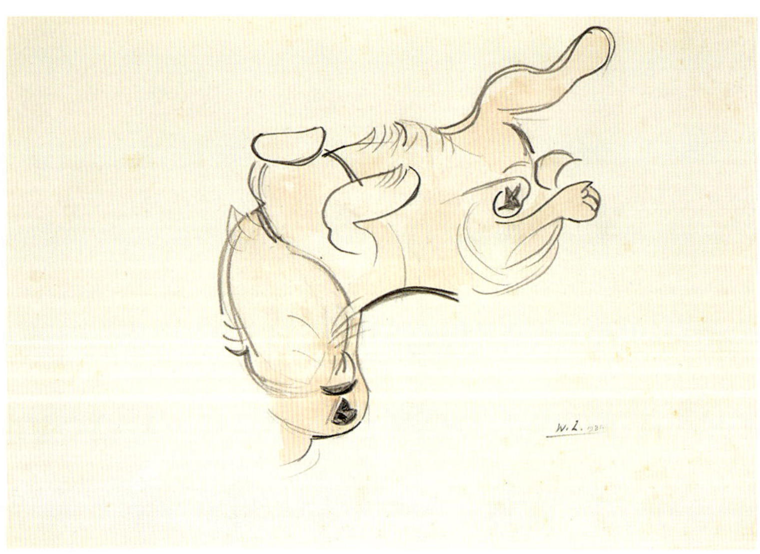

## 29 **HEAD AND PAWS OF TUT 1932**

Pencil on paper, 29.3 × 24.7 [M768]
Wyndham Lewis Memorial Trust:
G. and V. Lane collection

## 30 **THE SEAL DOG (TUT) 1931**

Pencil and watercolour on paper, 23.3 × 33.9
INSCRIPTIONS 'W.L. 1931.'; *verso*: 'The seal-dog'
Wyndham Lewis Memorial Trust:
Fitzpatrick bequest

## 31 **THE DUC DE JOYEUX SINGS 1932–33**

Pencil on paper, 30.2 × 18 [M662]
INSCRIPTIONS 'The Duc de Joyeux Sings' over 'Le Duc de Joyeux Sings' (erased) and 'W.L.'
EXHIBITED *Wyndham Lewis*, Santa Barbara Museum of Art, Santa Barbara, 1957, no. 38; *Paintings and Books by Wyndham Lewis*, York University Art Gallery, Toronto, 1964, no. 57
Walter and Harriet Michel

Lewis's ability to satirise friends as well as enemies is evident in this caricature of the writer James Joyce (1882–1941), which has been said to parody Joyce's pretensions to aristocratic status. The two men's close friendship had cooled after Lewis's attack of Joyce's novel *Ulysses* in 1927.

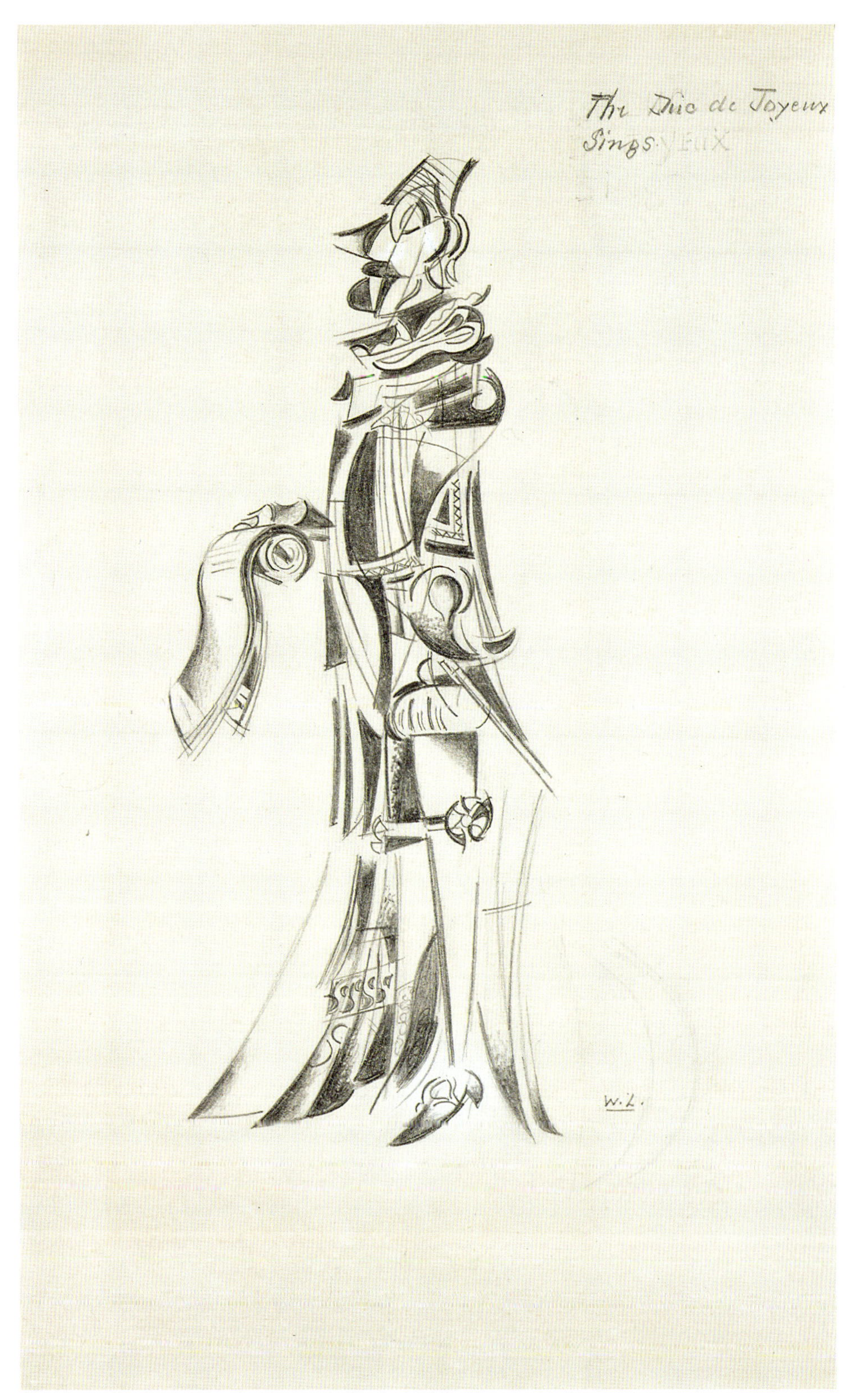
The Duc de Joyeux
Sings
W.L.

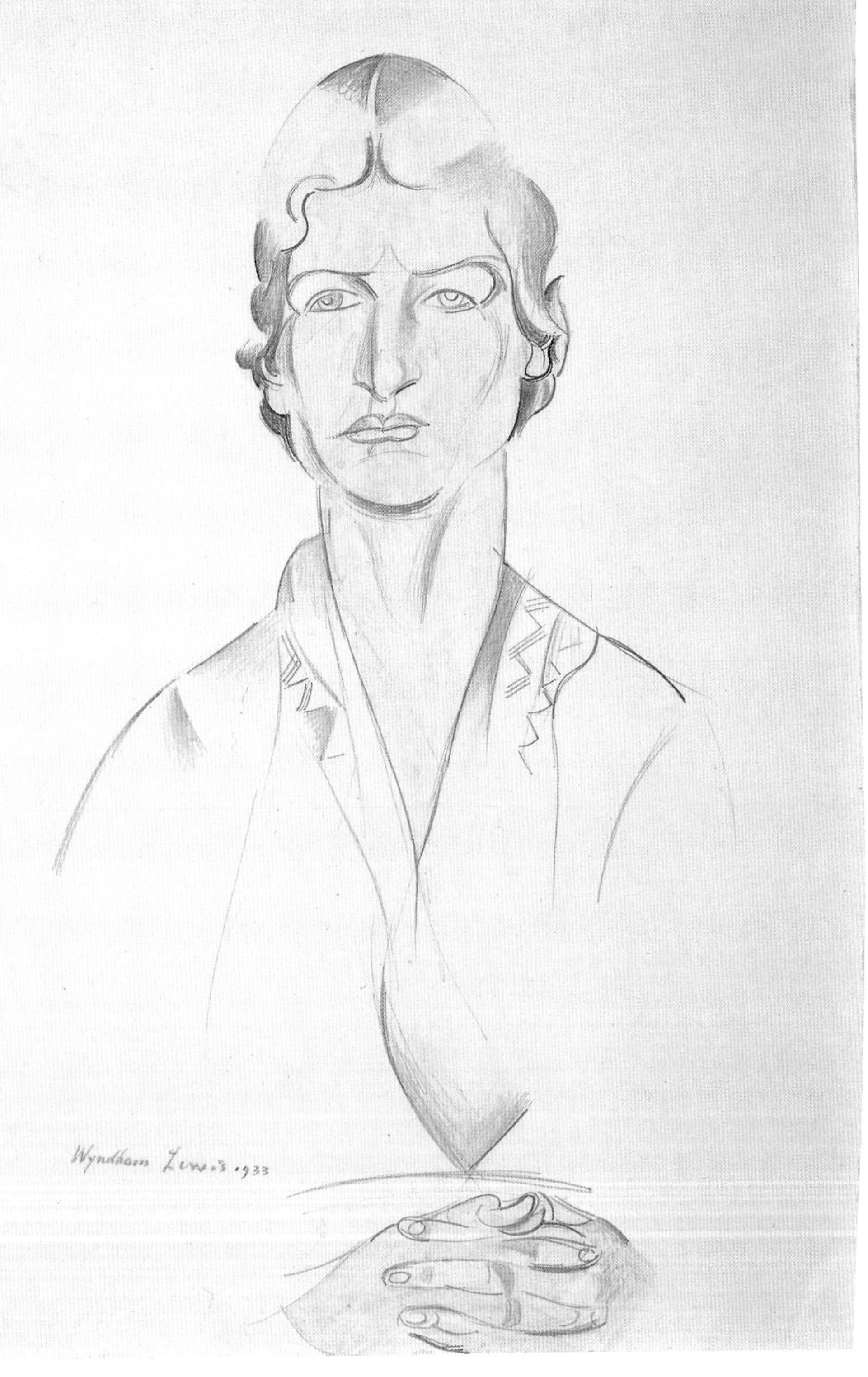
Wyndham Lewis 1933

## 32 SPARTAN PORTRAIT (NAOMI MITCHISON) 1933

Pencil and watercolour on paper, 39 x 26.7 [M809]
INSCRIPTIONS 'Wyndham Lewis 1933'; *verso*: 'Chieftaness.'
EXHIBITED *New Paintings and Drawings by Wyndham Lewis*, Beaux Arts Gallery, London, 1938, ex. cat.
Wyndham Lewis Memorial Trust: G. and V. Lane collection

## 33 HEAD OF A YOUNG WOMAN 1936

Pencil on paper, 34.7 x 32.6 [M603]
INSCRIPTION 'W Lewis'
Private collection

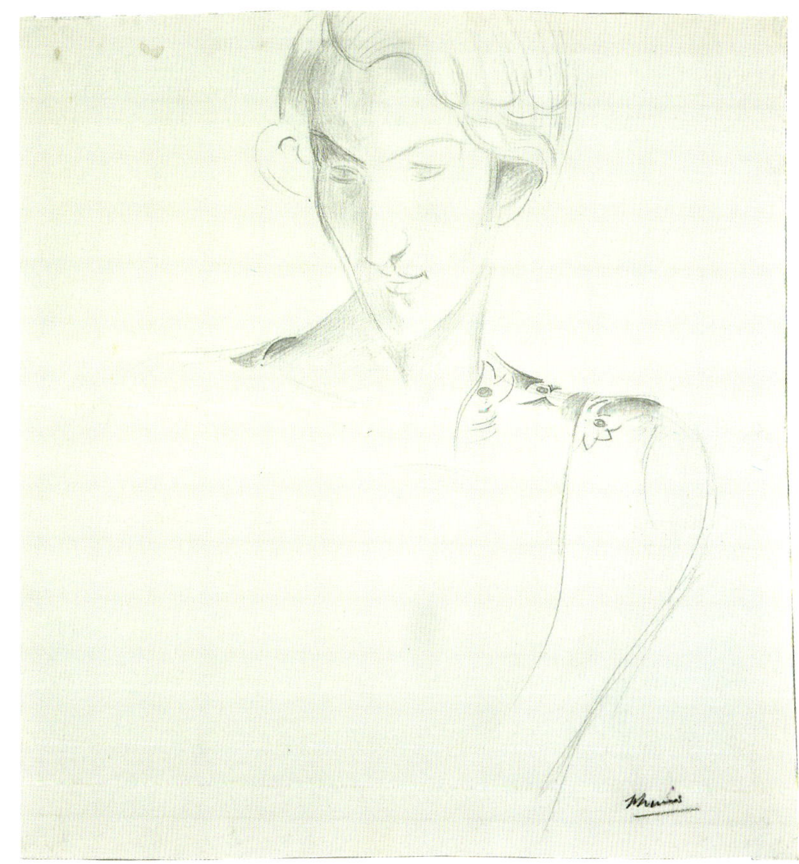

During the 1920s and '30s Lewis was a prolific portraitist. Indeed, T.G. Rosenthal commented that 'when one wants to recall the real face of the English intelligentsia between the wars it is Lewis's images which invariably appear on the retina'.[1] While many of his sitters, such as the figure in *Head of a Young Woman* (right), remain unknown, *Spartan Portrait* (left) is clearly identifiable as one of fifteen drawings Lewis made of the Scottish writer Naomi Mitchison (1897–1999). Lewis felt this drawing was a prime example of his best work from nature, reproducing it in the essay 'Super-nature versus Super-real', which prefaced his autobiography of 1939.

Mitchison met Lewis in the early 1930s, having written a positive review of his novel *The Apes of God* for *Time and Tide*, a feminist magazine to which she regularly contributed. Lewis illustrated Mitchison's book *Beyond this Limit* in 1935 and Mitchison became a great supporter of Lewis, purchasing his work and providing him with fruitful contacts. She was among the artists and writers who signed a letter to *The Times* in 1937 to promote public recognition of Lewis's art. Lewis appears to have had an intellectually equal friendship with Mitchison, often discussing philosophy and politics in his correspondence with her.

This drawing captures Mitchison in a serious mood and her upright posture and direct gaze reflect the inscription 'Chieftaness' made by Lewis on the reverse of the sheet. This may also refer to her Scottish heritage: Mitchison moved to the Highlands in 1937, living there until her death. LA

NOTE

1. T.G. Rosenthal, 'Introduction', *Word and Image 1 & 2: Wyndham Lewis and Michael Ayrton*, National Book League, London, 1971, p. 8.

## 34 **FOUR FIGURES IN A LANDSCAPE 1935?**

Pencil, pen and ink, watercolour and gouache on paper,
38.1 x 27.8
INSCRIPTION 'Wyndham Lewis 193[5?]'
Wyndham Lewis Memorial Trust: Fox collection

*Four Figures in a Landscape* exemplifies Lewis's fascination during the mid-1930s with history, myth and exploration. In particular it makes direct reference to his interest in the Norsemen, warfaring conquerors who had invaded western Europe in the ninth and tenth centuries. There was widespread interest in the subject of Norse history in the 1930s, particularly after the publication in 1937 of W.H. Auden and Louis MacNeice's *Letters from Iceland*. Lewis had already begun to pursue the theme in both his visual and his literary work, characterising the Norsemen in his 1938 book *The Mysterious Mr Bull* as 'ferocious, seagoing, playboys', 'big bloodthirsty Scandinavian schoolboys, fair, flaxen, and fierce, with unwieldy big pink bodies, and a fixed idea of cut-throat fun, never tired of bludgeons and battle-axes. They were the sinister Peter Pans of the land of frostbite and white-nights'.[1]

In this drawing the Norse explorers are brought vividly to life as they disembark from their sailing ship and begin their swashbuckling journey into foreign territory. Lewis allies historical references such as the Viking ship with more whimsical, imaginative details, from the figures' peculiar hooded costumes to the barren landscape, strewn with bizarre rectangular forms. The strong diagonal composition emphasises the warriors' strident march forward. Using black ink to delineate the figures, Lewis employs watercolour washes to enliven the drawing, picking out a rocky mound at the left and the ice-capped, moonlit peaks in the distance. In subject-matter and composition *Four Figures in a Landscape* relates closely to Lewis's painting of around 1936–37, *Landscape with Northmen* (M P66, private collection), where similarly horned figures appear in a compact row, the prow of a ship, as here, suggesting their recent arrival on shore.

Lewis's interest in the Norse warriors, like his admiration for the Berber people following a visit to Morocco in 1931 (see cat. 27 and 28), seems to reflect a fascination for foreign lands and their peoples. Yet for Lewis the Norsemen were not simply foreigners, Scandinavians or Danes from far-flung lands. In *The Mysterious Mr Bull* he devoted an entire chapter to the role of these Northern warriors in the making of Britain, arguing that, like the Saxons and Slavs, they formed one of the key [ingredients] for the "British" broth'.[2] Thus *Four Figures in a Landscape* might be seen as one of the series of mythological history pictures which, like Lewis's 1937 painting *The Armada* (M P70, Vancouver Art Gallery), alluded to epic chapters in British history.

The precise dating of *Four Figures in a Landscape* is unclear. In an article of 1987 the drawing's owner, C.J. Fox, proposed a dating of 1938 on the basis of stylistic similarities in the handling of the landscape with two other drawings of that year, and because 1938 has been seen as the climax of Lewis's interest in the theme of Norse explorations, even as his 'Viking year'.[3] Fox went on to suggest that the drawing might be one of Lewis's 'missing' works, exhibited at the Beaux Arts Gallery in London in 1938, entitled *Norsk* or 'Norse'. Yet Lewis's interest in the Vikings, as other paintings and drawings attest, began earlier in the 1930s. Furthermore, while the date, inscribed in the rocks at the lower left, is partially blurred, it appears to read '1935'. JK

NOTES

1 Wyndham Lewis, *The Mysterious Mr Bull*, Robert Hale, London, 1938, pp. 53 and 55.
2 *Ibid.*, p. 56.
3 C.J. Fox, 'A "Lost" Lewis Found?', *Enemy News*, no. 24, 1987, p. 5.

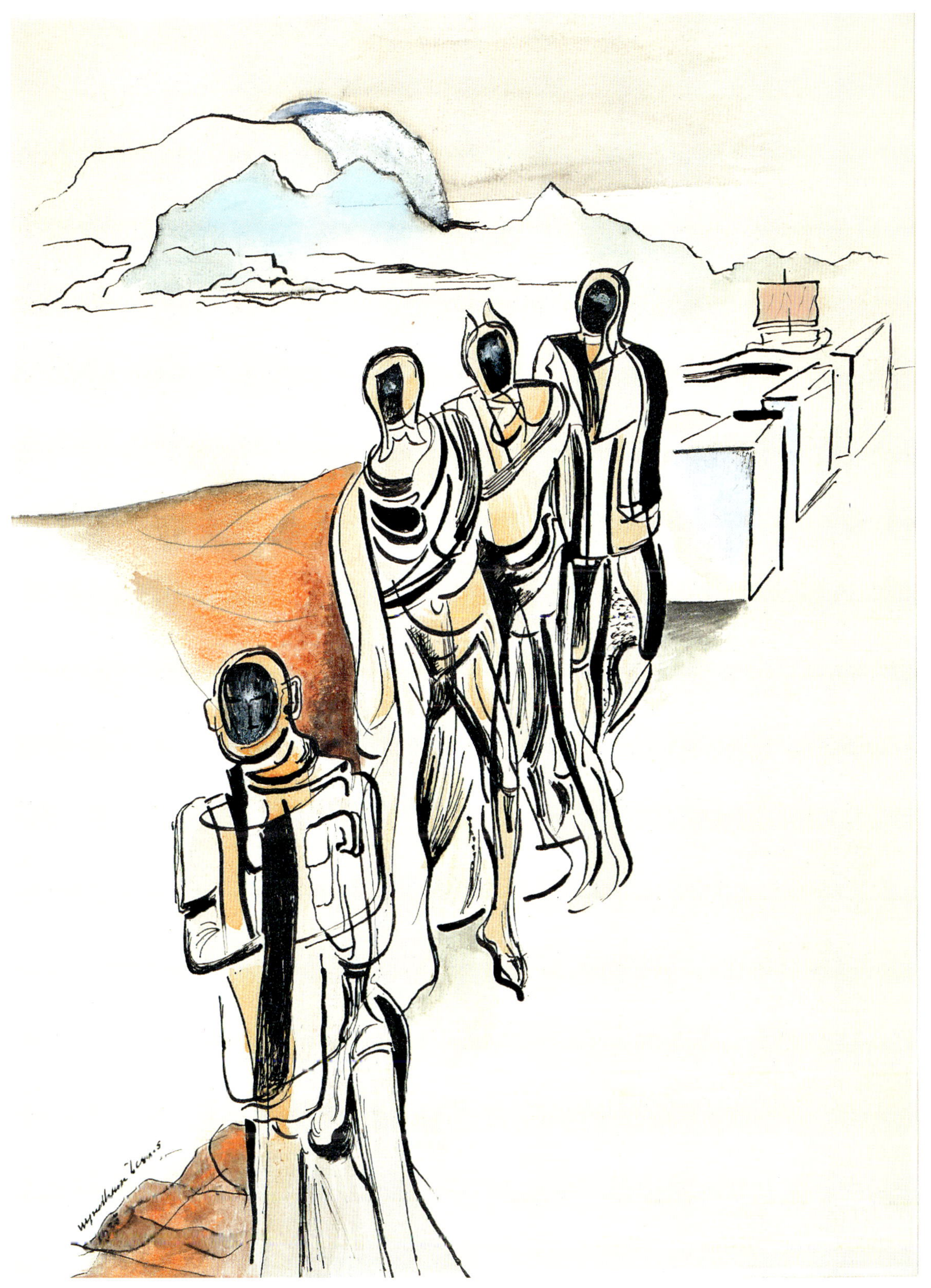

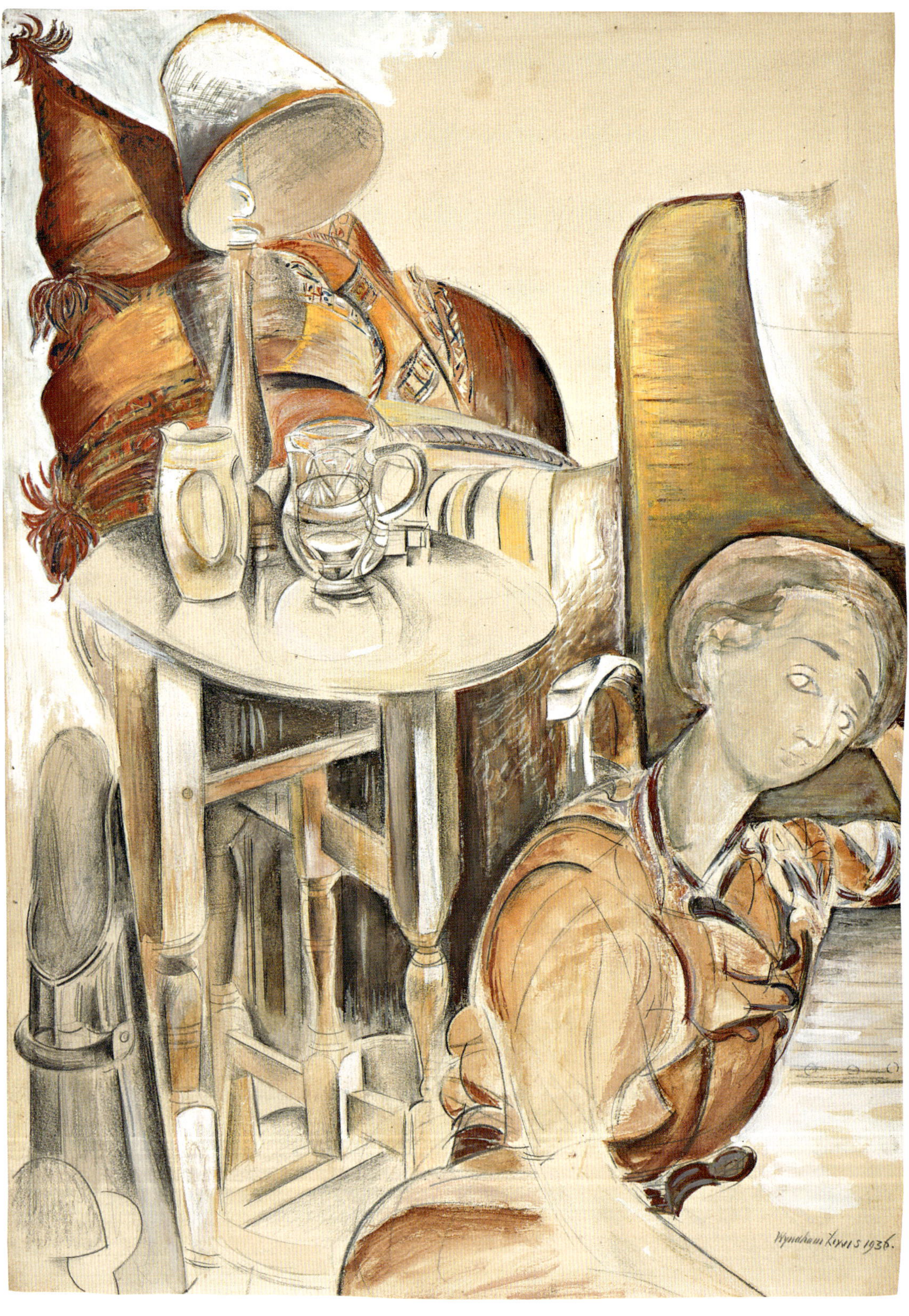
Wyndham Lewis 1936.

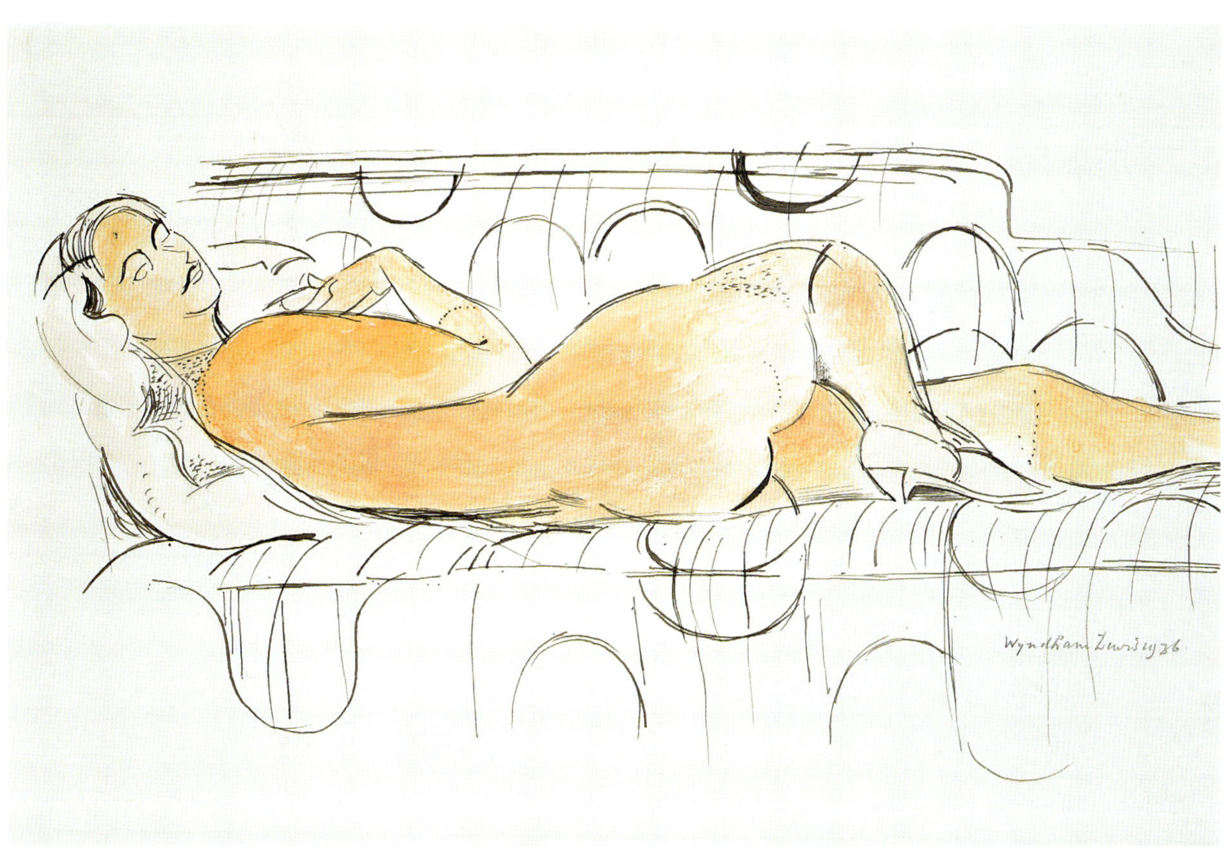


35 **THE ROOM 1936**

Pencil, chalk, watercolour and gouache on paper, 49.9 × 35.4 [M872]
INSCRIPTIONS 'Wyndham Lewis 1936.'
Private collection

36 **NUDE ON SOFA 1936**

Pen and ink and watercolour on paper, 32.8 × 36.5 (full sheet); 24.9 × 36.5 (as shown) [M862]
INSCRIPTIONS 'Wyndham Lewis 1936.'; *verso*: 'Nude on sofa (2)'
Walter and Harriet Michel

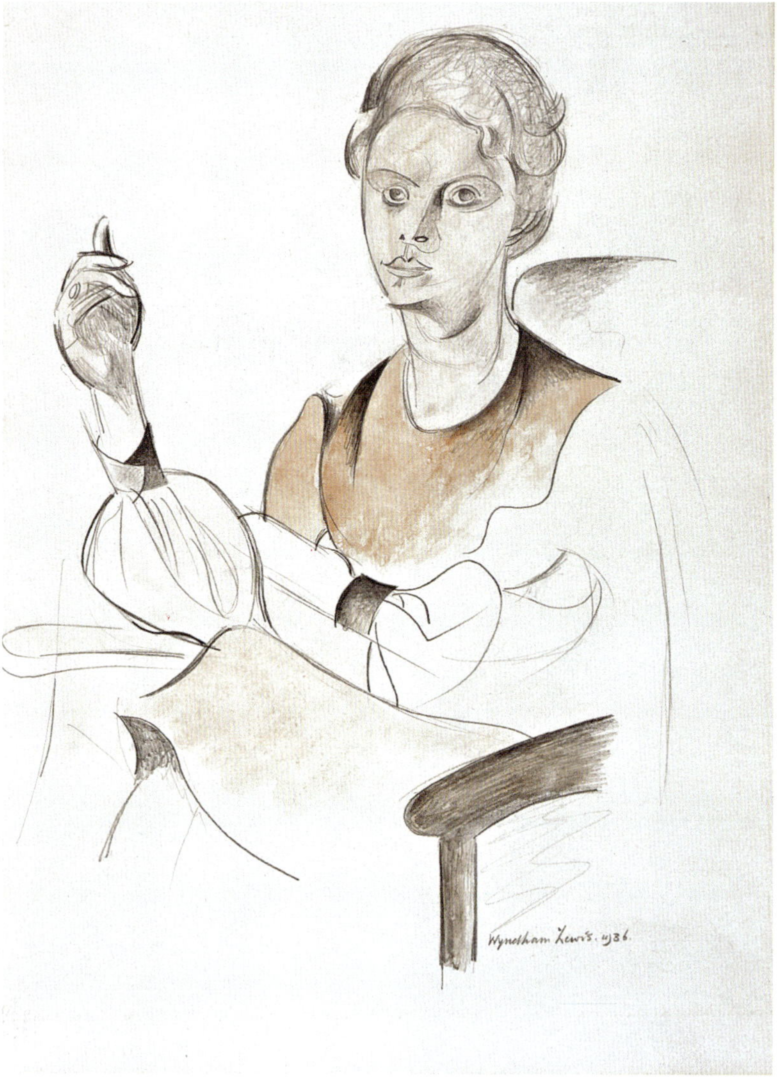

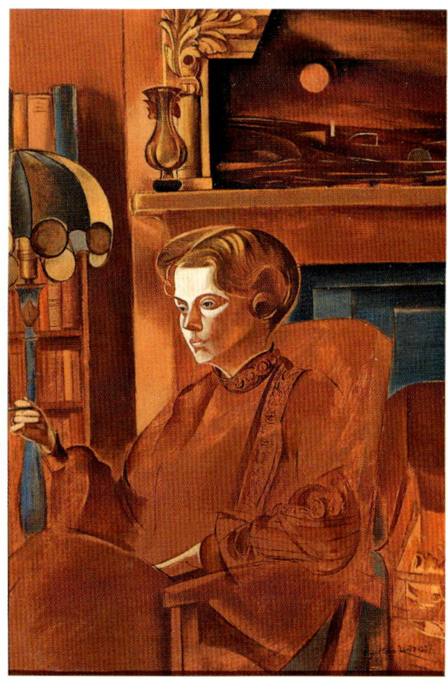

*Red Portrait*, 1937, oil on canvas, 93 x 60 [M P76]
Wyndham Lewis Memorial Trust: G. and V. Lane collection

## 37 **YOUNG WOMAN SEATED 1936**

Pencil and watercolour on paper, 39.8 x 28.9 [M883]
INSCRIBED 'Wyndham Lewis. 1936.'
EXHIBITED *Wyndham Lewis*, Redfern Gallery, London, 1949, no. 93; *Wyndham Lewis and Vorticism*, Tate Gallery, London, 1956, no. 102
Private collection, London

## 38 **WOMAN WITH YELLOW HAIR 1936**

Pencil and watercolour on paper, 37.7 x 26.6 [M882]
INSCRIPTIONS 'Wyndham Lewis 1936'
Private collection

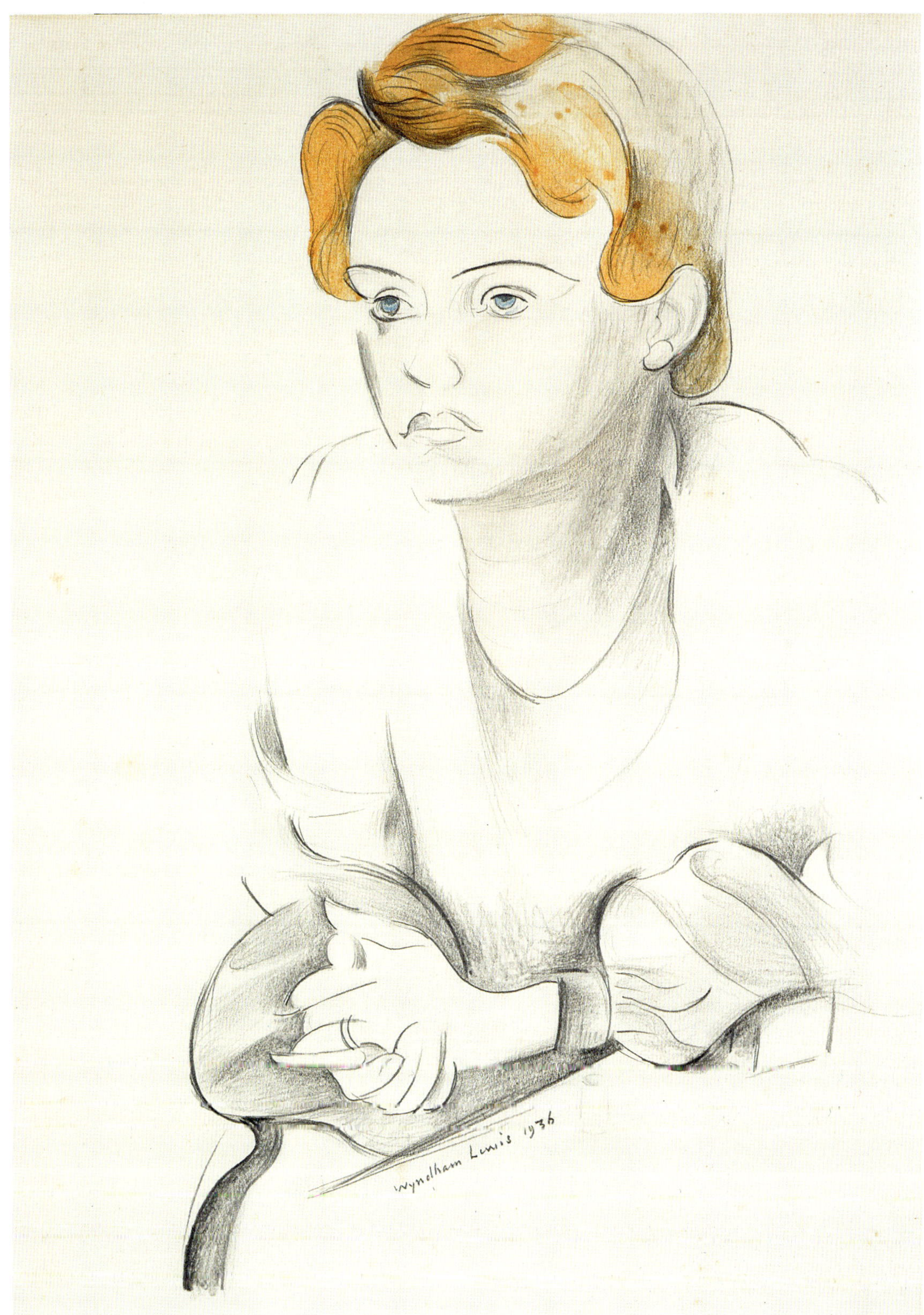
Wyndham Lewis 1936

## 39 **THE ARTIST'S WIFE 1938**

Pencil, pen and ink and watercolour on paper, 35.5 x 25.2 [M897]
INSCRIPTIONS 'Wyndham Lewis 1938.'; *verso:* 'A portrait, New Year 1938.'
Wyndham Lewis Memorial Trust: Fox collection

Lewis met Gladys Anne Hoskins (1900–79) in 1918 and the two lived together from 1921, only marrying on 9 October 1930. Gladys became known as 'Froanna', a humorous corruption of 'Frau Anna', an address which had been used by a German friend. For many years Lewis insisted on keeping their marriage a secret, failing to introduce her to his friends and acquaintances, and assigning her the role of tea-maker and cook. She was rarely seen by visitors to his home; one friend apparently 'saw Froanna's disembodied hands appear through the serving hatch for many years before he actually met her'.[1] Lewis had expressed strongly anti-feminist views in his 1926 book *The Art of Being Ruled*, which seem to reflect this attitude. However, Froanna was surprised at the suggestion that Lewis was hostile to women, saying: 'Was Lewis anti-women? Some cheek, a womanizer like that!'[2] Despite his philandering nature, and their sometimes turbulent marriage, Lewis clearly felt true affection for Froanna. Indeed, she was his muse, both in literary and visual terms. She emerges as the principal figure of Margot in his 1937 novel *The Revenge for Love*, and appears in numerous drawings, either as the identified subject or the unnamed model. Her presence in Lewis's life was critical during the 1930s, when she cared for him through a number of serious illnesses. During a near-fatal attack in 1934, Lewis asked a friend to look after 'my very much loved wife, Gladys Anne'.[3]

It was during their prolonged stay in North America throughout the Second World War that Froanna took on a more public role in Lewis's life. In a letter to John Rothenstein's wife in December 1939 Lewis wrote that 'life has been somewhat of a war for me, and the warrior – the Gauls being an exception – has usually kept the field of battle free of females. Man's domestic nature is stressed here in your American matriarchy and I have found myself rather overshadowed by my wife, as a fact, and she has been forced a little into the fray.'[4]

Four drawings of Froanna are reproduced here, all made between 1936 and 1938. *Woman with Yellow Hair* (cat. 38) and *Young Woman seated* (cat. 37) form part of a series of drawings produced during 1936 in which Froanna wears the same full-sleeved blouse, and which may be preparatory studies for one of his most important and striking late oils, *Red Portrait* (illus. p. 72). In contrast to these more pensive images, in *Nude on Sofa* (cat. 36), Froanna reclines alluringly, while *The Artist's Wife*, made at New Year, 1938, presents us with a formidable, glamorous woman. In later years Froanna would recall that this drawing was an image she particularly liked. As well as depicting her femininity, Lewis makes a point of drawing her wedding band, as he does in *Woman with Yellow Hair*, and in doing so seems to reiterate her wifely status. These very different portraits of Froanna attest to Lewis's dependence on her, and the important role she played in his life. In 1939 he wrote that Froanna was not only 'a great reader of my books: but … a wife in a thousand'.[5] LA

NOTES

1. This was Hugh Porteus: see Jeffrey Meyers, *The Enemy: A Biography of Wyndham Lewis*, Routledge & Kegan Paul, London and Henley, 1980, p. 100.
2. Quoted *ibid.*, p. 100.
3. Lewis to Nicholas Waterhouse, quoted *ibid.*, p. 101.
4. Letter to Mrs John Rothenstein, December 1939, *The Letters of Wyndham Lewis*, ed. W.K. Rose, Methuen, London, 1963, p. 269.
5. *Ibid.*, p. 269.

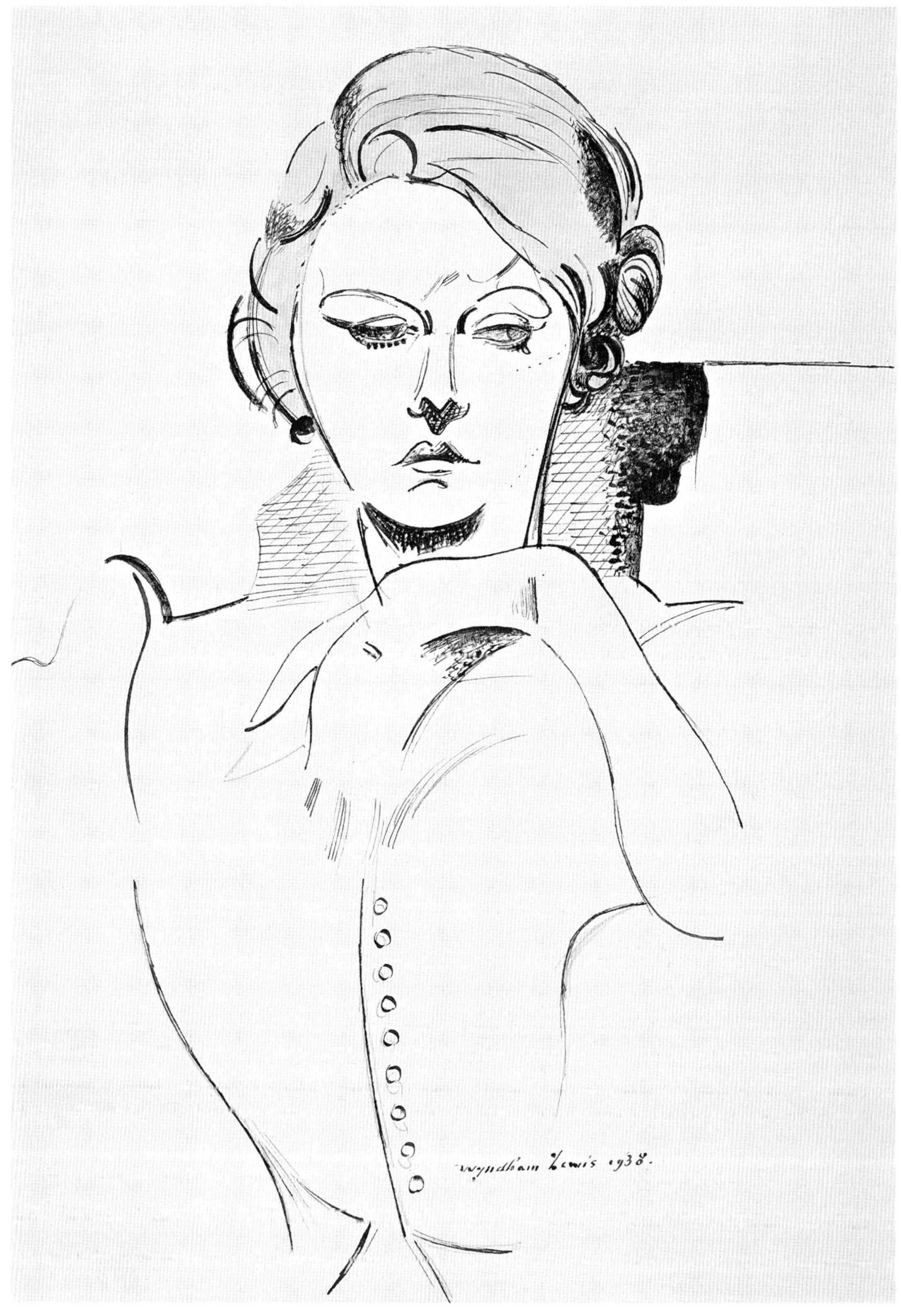
Wyndham Lewis 1938.

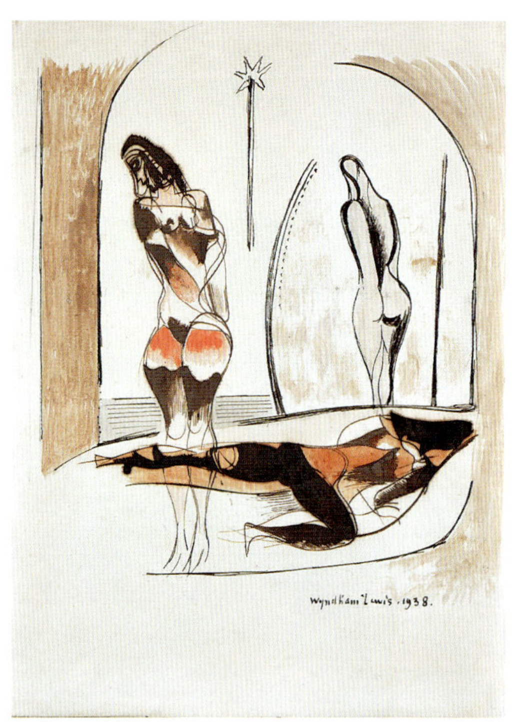

## 40 SEA CAVE 1938

Pen and ink, ink wash and gouache on paper, 27.4 x 19.8 [M921]

INSCRIPTION 'Wyndham Lewis. 1938.'

EXHIBITED *Wyndham Lewis*, Zwemmer Gallery, London, 1957, no. 32; *Paintings and Books by Wyndham Lewis*, York University Art Gallery, Toronto, 1964, no. 58

Walter and Harriet Michel

## 41 MEETING OF SHEIKS 1938

Pencil, pen and ink, watercolour and gouache on paper, 25.3 x 35.9 [M908]

INSCRIPTIONS 'Wyndham Lewis 1938'

EXHIBITED *Wyndham Lewis*, Zwemmer Gallery, London, 1957, no. 7

Walter and Harriet Michel

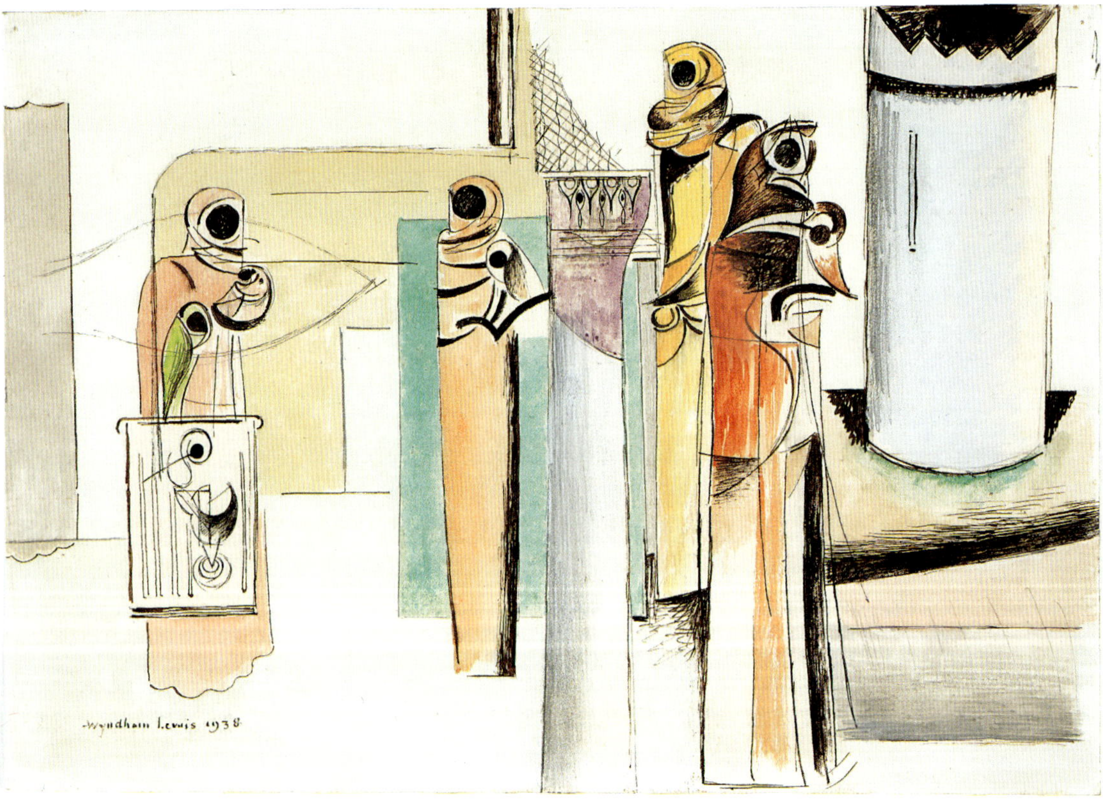

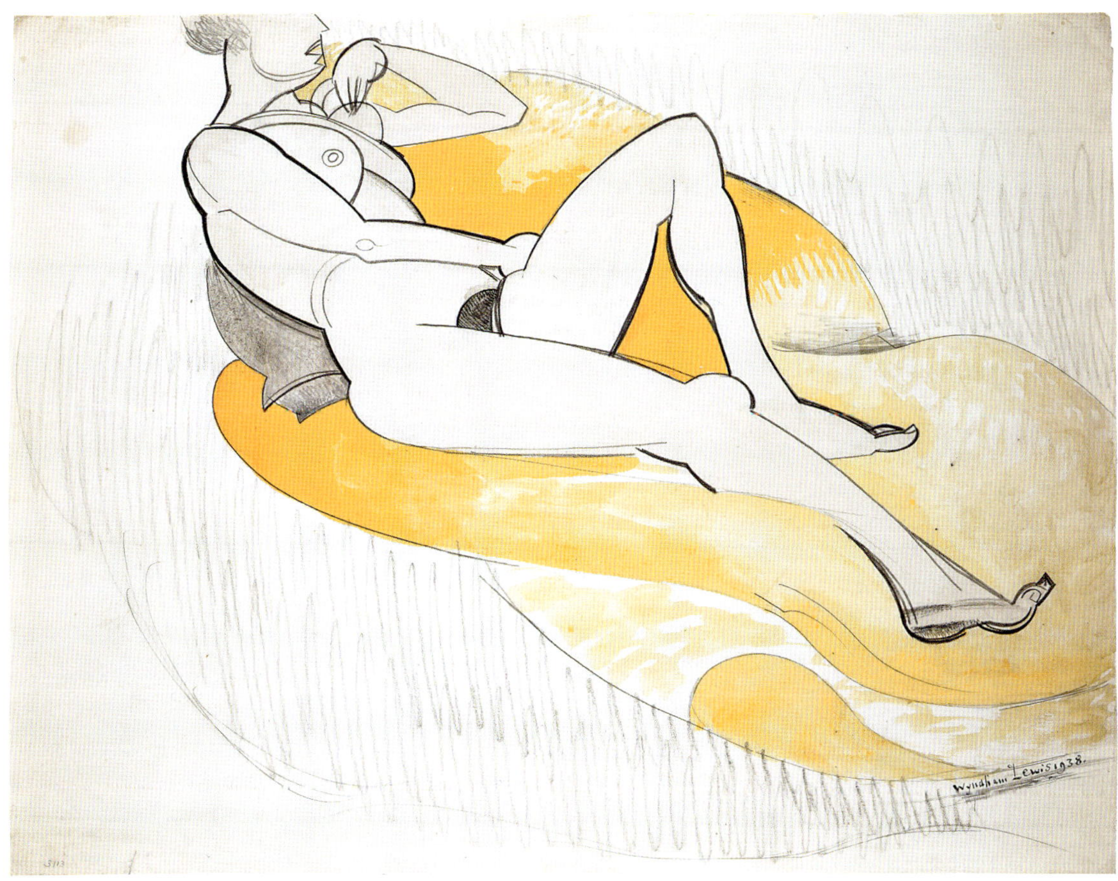


42 **NUDE 1938 (probably started c. 1919)**

Pencil, pen and ink, chalk and watercolour on paper, 38.1 × 49.6
[M915]
INSCRIPTIONS 'Wyndham Lewis 1938.' over partly erased earlier signature with date scratched out; *verso*: 'nude'
Walter and Harriet Michel

Although signed and dated 1938, another inscription obscured below suggests that this drawing was begun at an earlier date. Indeed, the subject of the female nude and the strong contouring of the woman's body are reminiscent of the figure studies Lewis made after the First World War, when he moved away from geometric abstraction and returned to working from nature (see *Reclining Nude*, cat. 15). His idiom remained emphatically modern, and in this drawing we find his innovative approach in the stylised treatment of both the woman's anatomy and the *chaise longue* on which she reclines. The work was completed in the same year that Lewis was making fantastical and highly coloured drawings such as *Bathing Scene* (cat. 43). However, here, the wash of yellow watercolour is used decoratively, illuminating the figure and the virtuosity of Lewis's draughtsmanship. LA

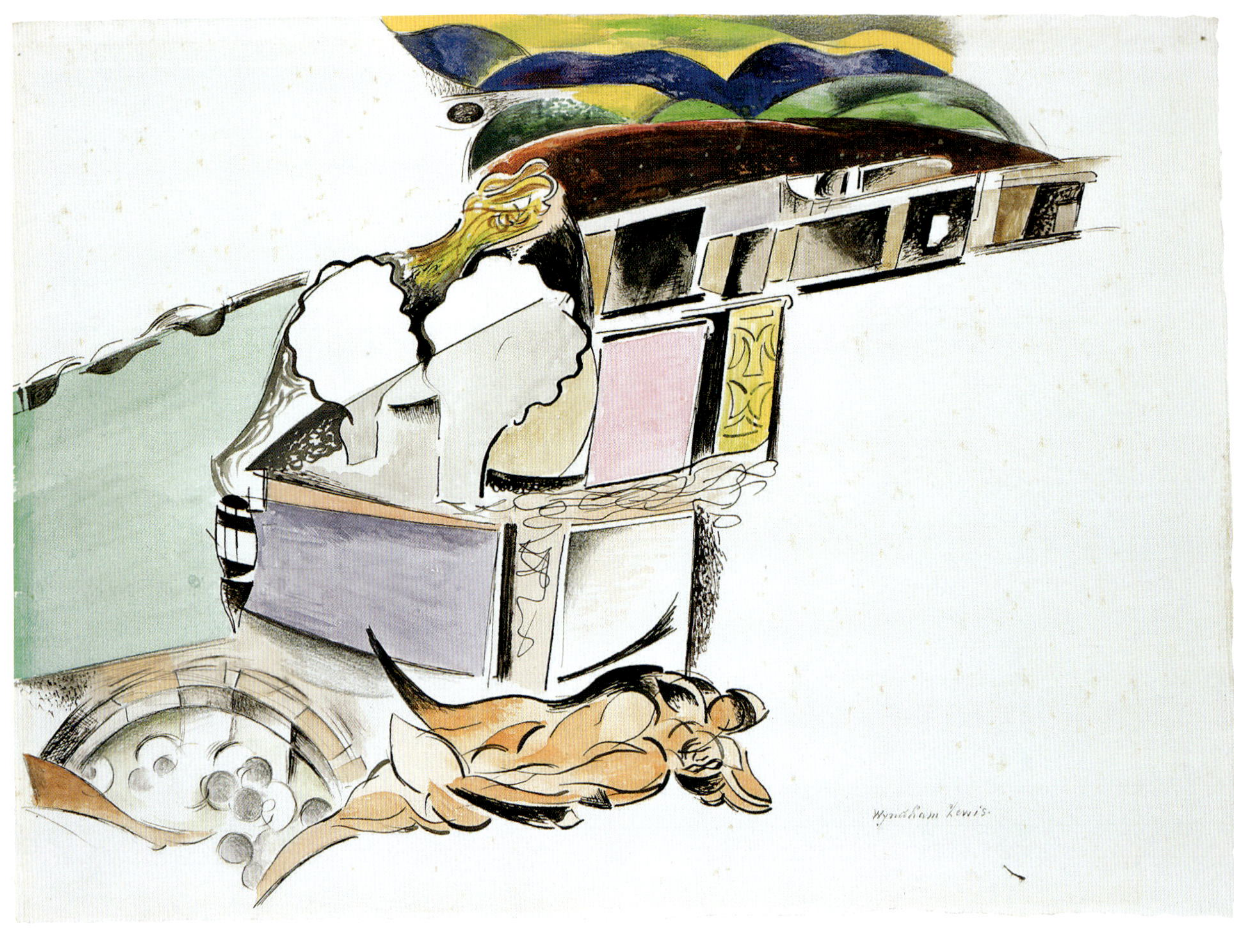


## 43 BATHING SCENE 1938

Pen and ink, watercolour and gouache on paper, 28.7 × 39.6 [M900]
INSCRIPTION 'Wyndham Lewis.'
EXHIBITED *Wyndham Lewis*, Zwemmer Gallery, London, 1957, no. 11; *Paintings and Books by Wyndham Lewis*, York University Art Gallery, Toronto, 1964, no. 59
Walter and Harriet Michel

In the 1930s Lewis's work increasingly alluded to literary, historical and mythological sources, to metaphysics and the world of the imagination. In *Bathing Scene* Lewis creates an enigmatic fantasy, as a couple lie embracing in the foreground while a complex cascade of abstract forms appears above them, receding into the distance. A bridge over a foaming river at the lower left might suggest a journey into the realms of imagination or desire. Lewis's skills as a colourist are brilliantly demonstrated here, as fields of subdued aquamarine, rose and violet watercolour contrast with the more strident gouache tones in the upper part of the drawing. JK

*right above*

## 44 '... AND WILDERNESS WERE PARADISE ENOW' 1941

Chalk, watercolour and gouache on paper, 42.1 × 32 [M965]
INSCRIPTION 'W. Lewis. 1941'
EXHIBITED *Wyndham Lewis: Drawings and Watercolours*, Victoria College, University of Toronto, Toronto, 1950; *'The Talented Intruder'*, Art Gallery of Windsor, Ontario, 1992, no. 18 (and on tour: Glenbow Museum, Calgary; Art Gallery of Ontario, Toronto, 1993)
Private collection

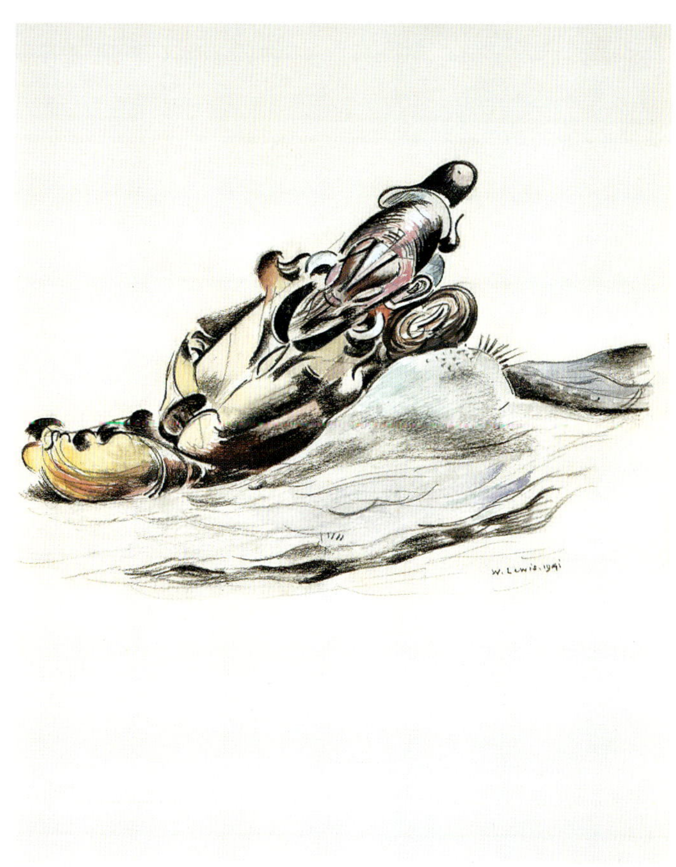

*below*

### 45 **A MAN'S FORMS TAKING A FALL FROM A SMALL HORSE 1941**

Pencil, pen and ink, watercolour and gouache on paper, 29.5 × 44.9 [M977]
INSCRIPTIONS 'Lewis. 1941.'; *verso:* 'A man's forms taking a fall from a small horse.'
EXHIBITED *Wyndham Lewis: Drawings and Watercolours,* Victoria College, University of Toronto, Toronto, 1950; *Wyndham Lewis,* Manchester City Art Gallery, Manchester, 1980, no. 150; *Wyndham Lewis: Art and War,* Imperial War Museum, London, 1992, no. 68; *'The Talented Intruder',* Art Gallery of Windsor, Ontario, 1992, no. 13 (and on tour: Glenbow Museum, Calgary; Art Gallery of Ontario, Toronto, 1993)
Wyndham Lewis Memorial Trust: Fox collection

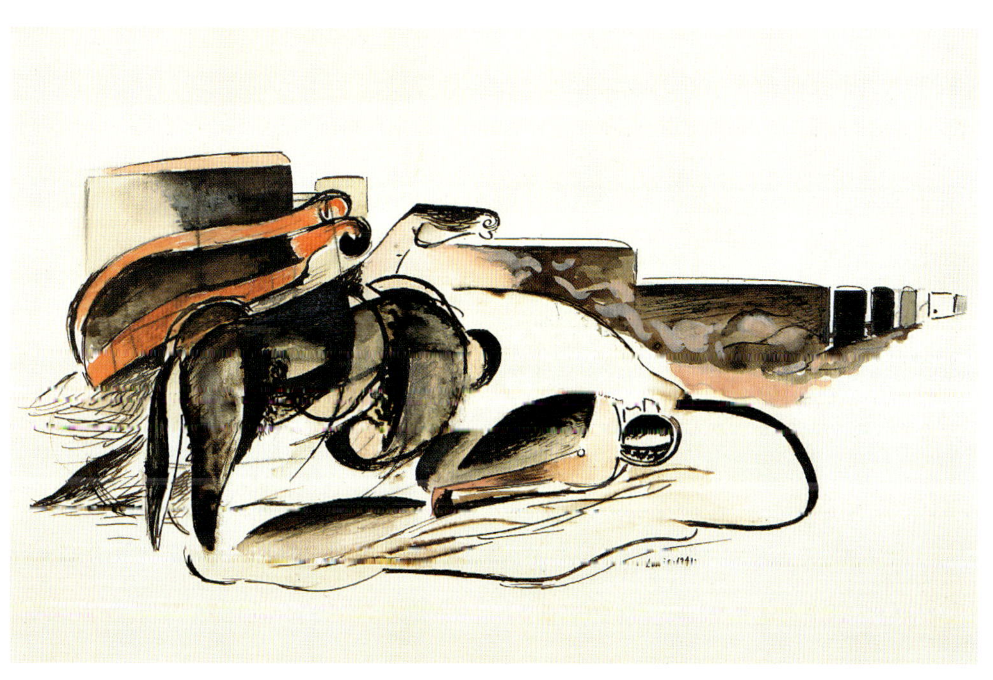

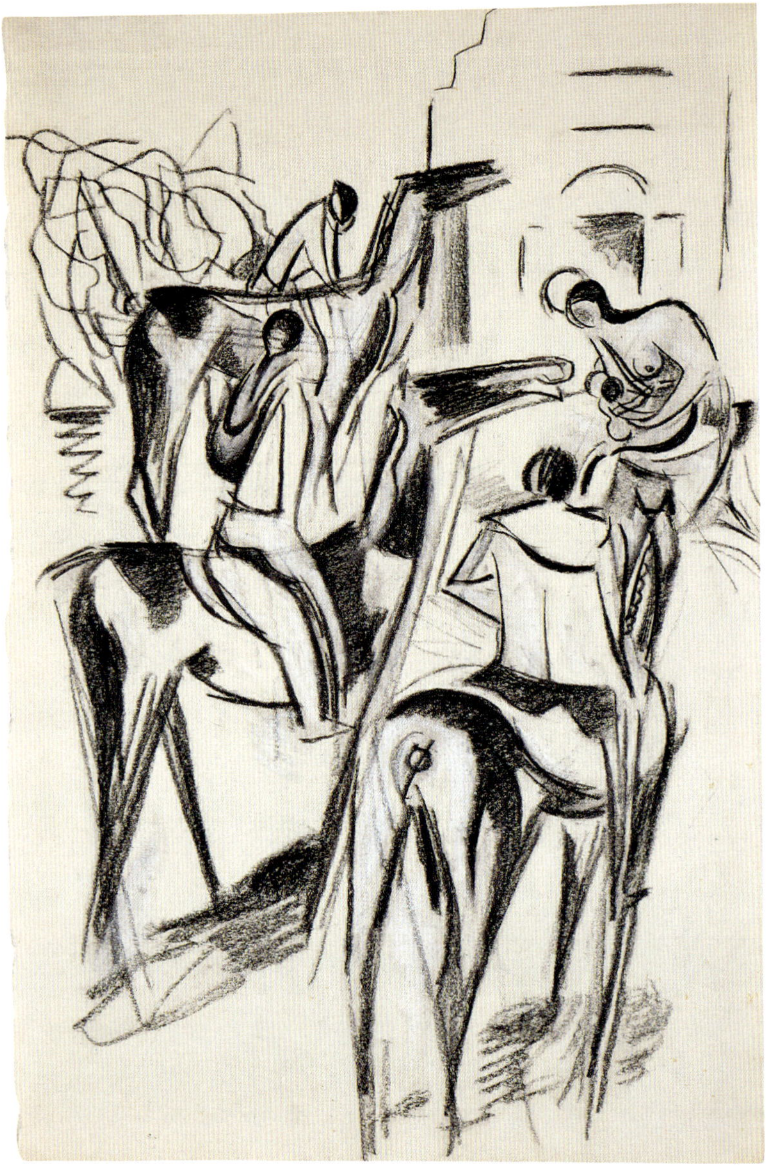

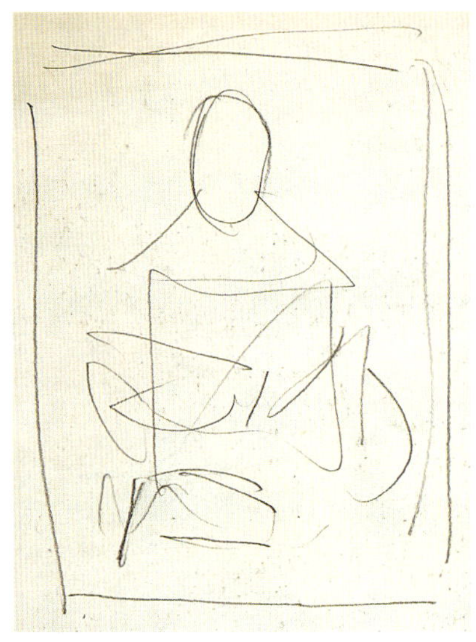

Verso (detail) of cat. 46

## 46 **ADORATION 1941**

Chalk and gouache on paper, 38 × 25.3
[M963]
EXHIBITED *'The Talented Intruder'*, Art Gallery of Windsor, Ontario, 1992, no. 21 (and on tour: Glenbow Museum, Calgary; Art Gallery of Ontario, Toronto, 1993)
Walter and Harriet Michel

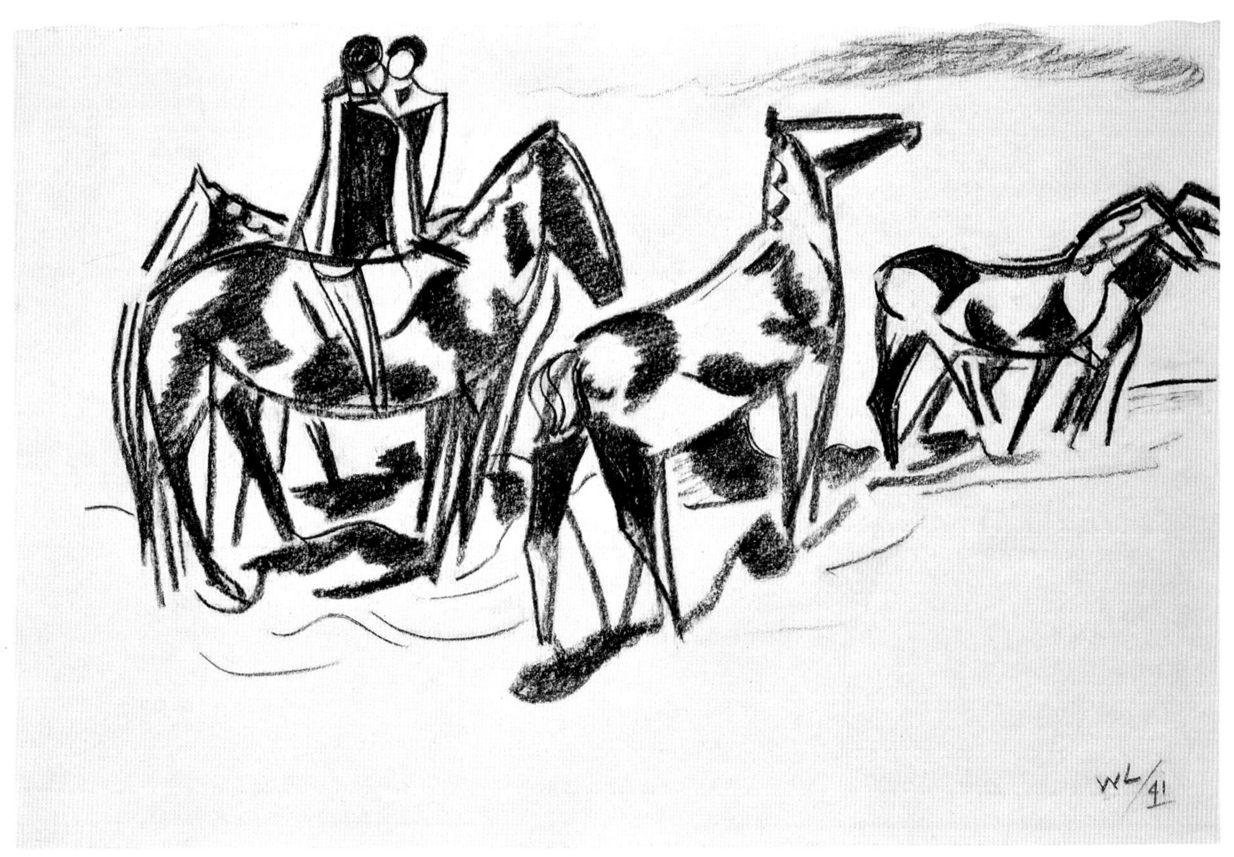


### 47 **HORSEMEN 1941**

Chalk on paper, 25.5 × 38.1 [M974]
INSCRIPTIONS 'WL/41'
EXHIBITED *'The Talented Intruder'*, Art Gallery of Windsor, Ontario, 1992, no. 12 (and on tour: Glenbow Museum, Calgary; Art Gallery of Ontario, Toronto, 1993)
Walter and Harriet Michel

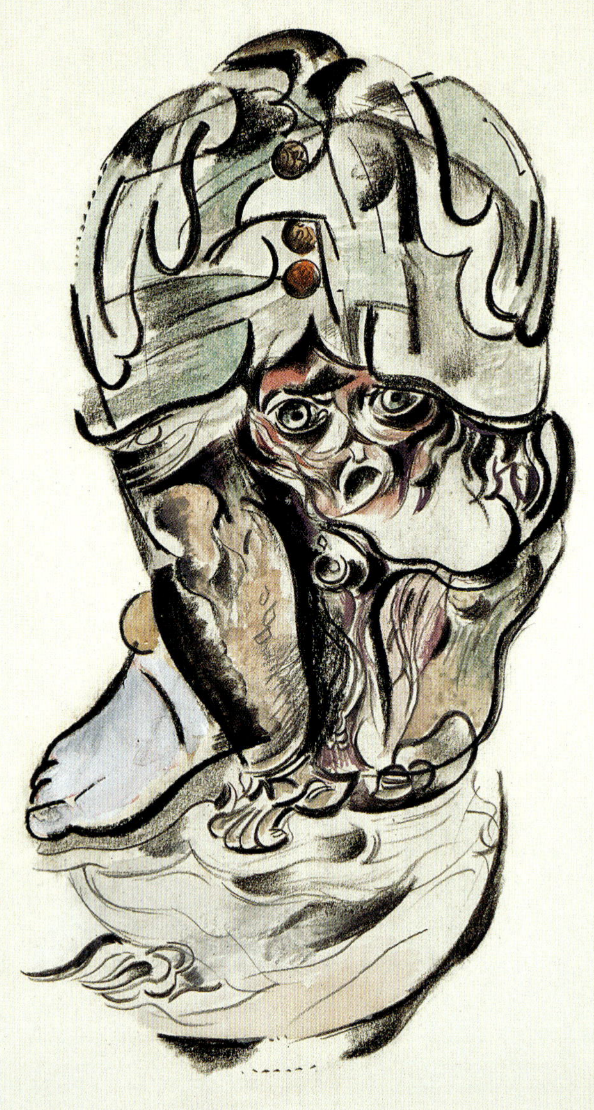

## 48 **LEBENSRAUM II: THE EMPTY TUNIC 1941–42**

Chalk, watercolour and gouache on paper, 34.6 x 24.3 [M988]
EXHIBITED *Wyndham Lewis: Drawings and Watercolours*, Victoria College, University of Toronto, Toronto, 1950; *Paintings and Books by Wyndham Lewis*, York University Art Gallery, Toronto, 1964, no. 33; *Wyndham Lewis: Art and War*, Imperial War Museum, London, 1992, no. 65
Wyndham Lewis Memorial Trust: G. and V. Lane collection

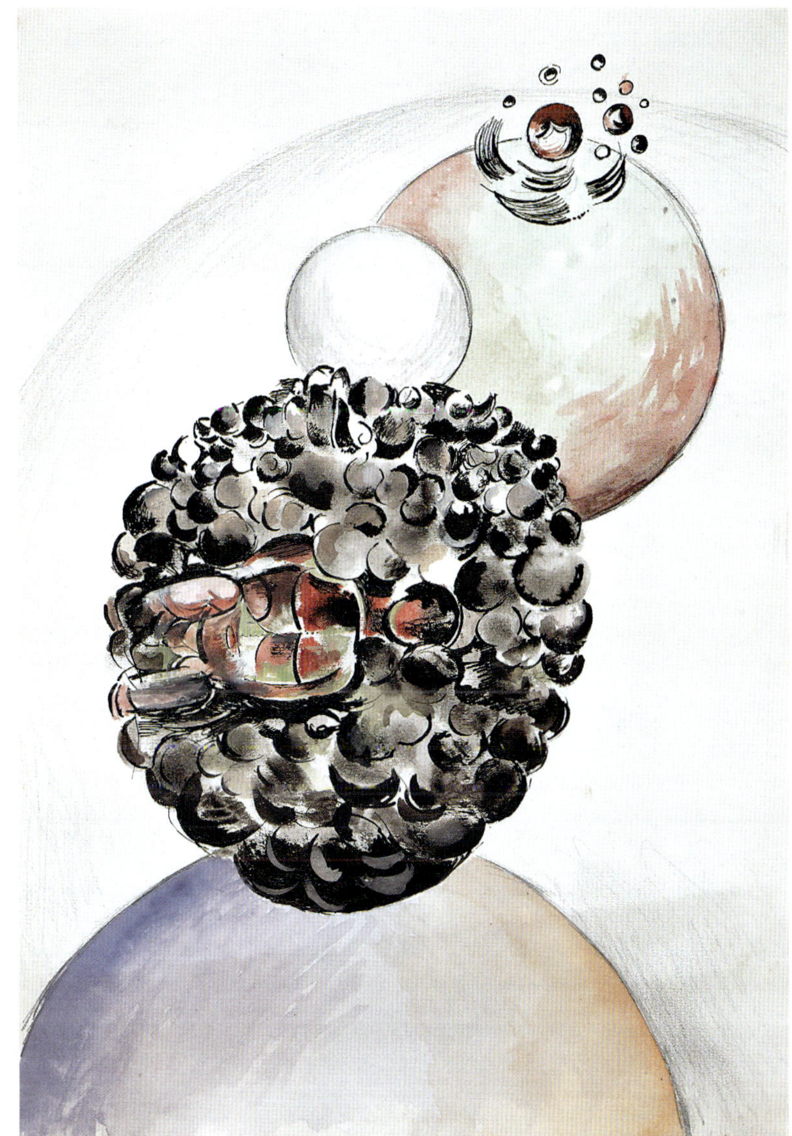

## 49 **CREATION MYTH 1941–42**

Pencil, pen and ink, watercolour and gouache on paper, 37 x 25.1 [M987]
EXHIBITED *'The Talented Intruder'*, Art Gallery of Windsor, Ontario, 1992, no. 28 (and on tour: Glenbow Museum, Calgary; Art Gallery of Ontario, Toronto, 1993)
Walter and Harriet Michel

The creation theme appeared in Lewis's work as early as 1912, when he exhibited a watercolour entitled *Creation* at the Second Post-Impressionist Exhibition, now only known through a photograph. He returned to the subject while in Canada, in a large group of drawings made during 1941 and '42 which he described as 'works of the imagination'.[1] The series encompassed a diverse range of subjects such as bathers, crucifixions and war (see, for example, cat. 48, left), all of which addressed the universal notions of the suffering and survival of the human race. In *Creation Myth*, an imaginary cosmic landscape is dominated by a multiplying, cellular form from which a figure emerges. This may represent God's creation of Adam, as described in Genesis. LA

NOTE

1. Letter to Theodore Spencer, 28 January 1942, quoted in *'The Talented Intruder'*, Art Gallery of Windsor, Ontario, 1992, p. 43.

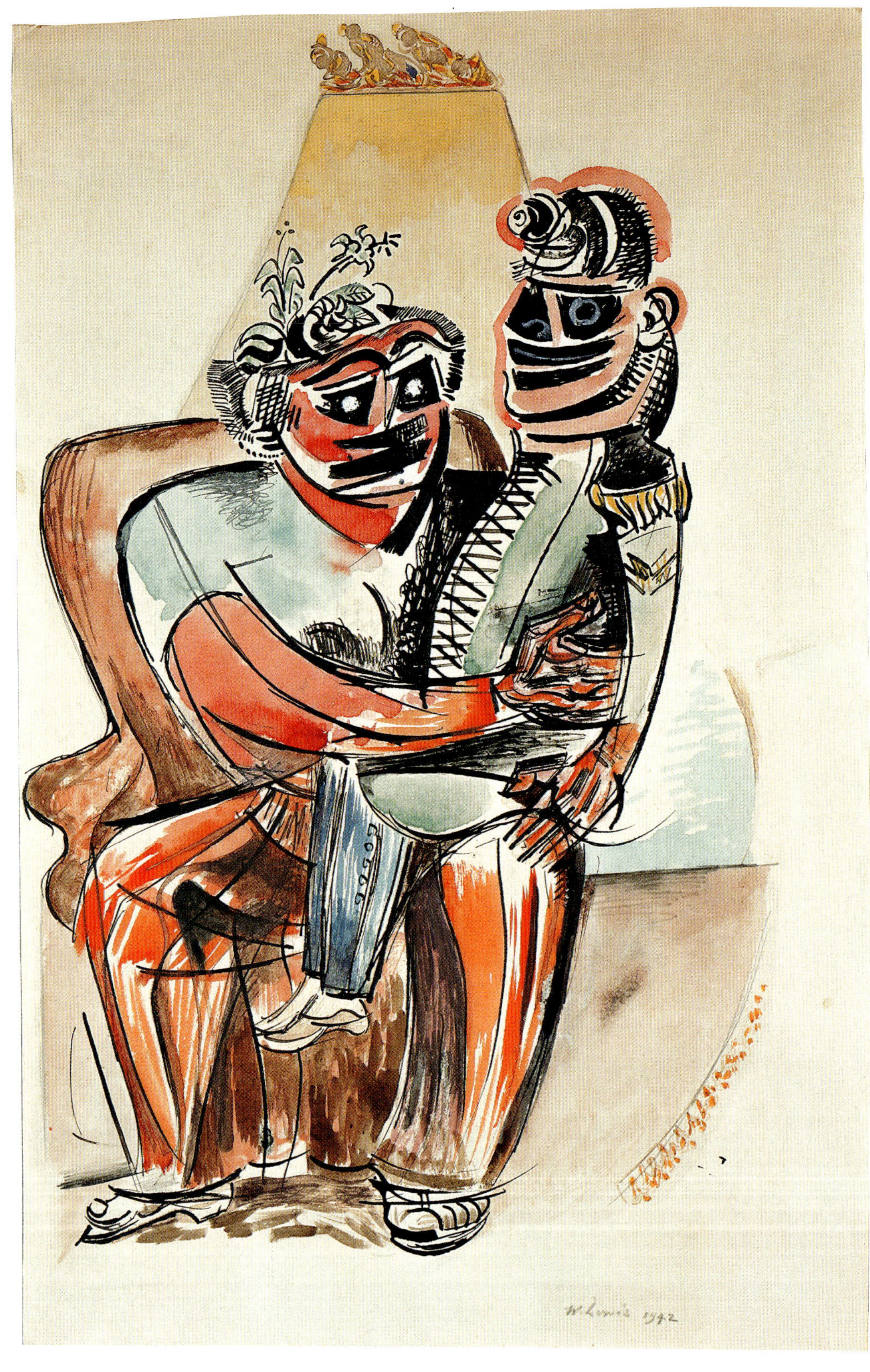
W. Lewis 1942

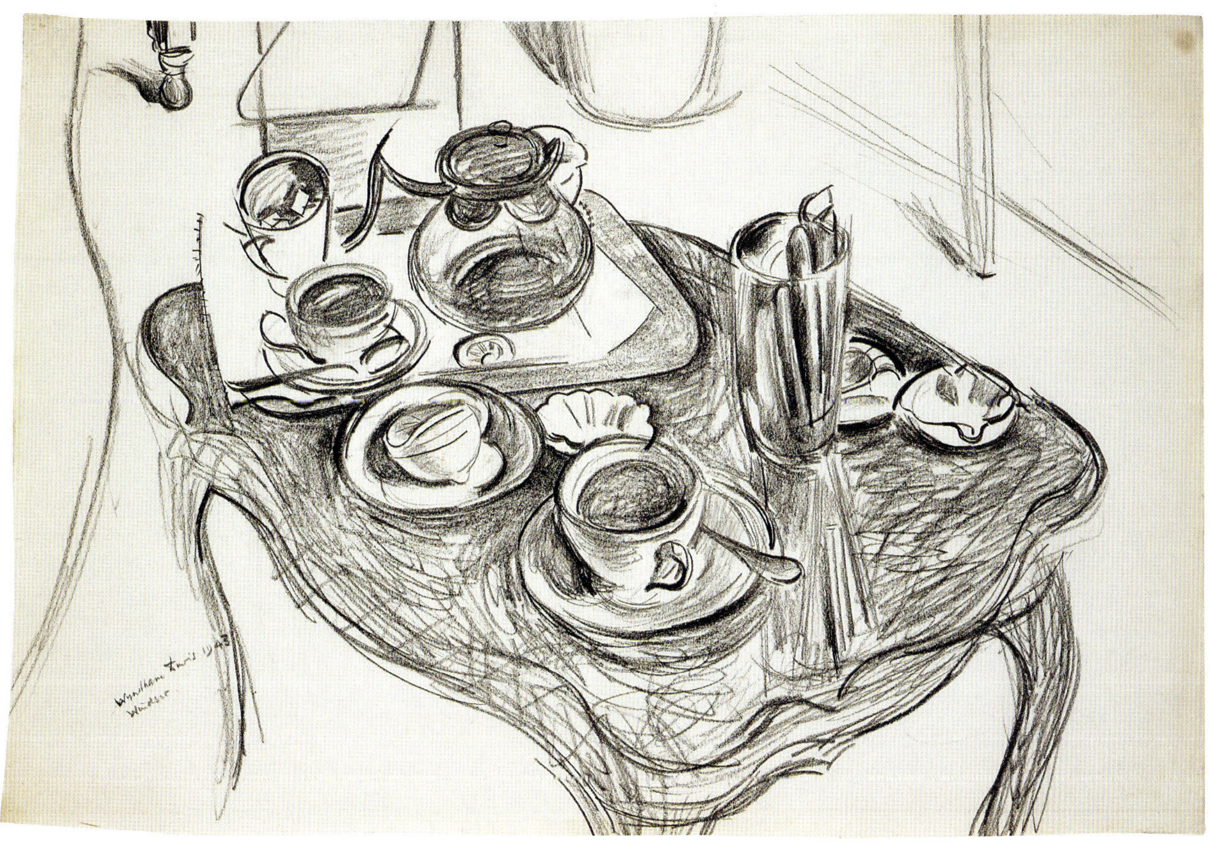

## 50 **MOTHER LOVE 1942**

Pencil, pen and ink, watercolour and gouache on paper, 43.6 × 28 [M998]
INSCRIPTIONS 'W. Lewis 1942'; *verso*: 'Mother-love'
EXHIBITED *Wyndham Lewis*, Santa Barbara Museum of Art, Santa Barbara, 1957, no. 39; *Wyndham Lewis: Art and War*, Imperial War Museum, London, 1992, no. 71; *'The Talented Intruder'*, Art Gallery of Windsor, Ontario, 1992, no. 42 (and on tour: Glenbow Museum, Calgary; Art Gallery of Ontario, Toronto, 1993)
Walter and Harriet Michel

## 51 **TABLE WITH TRAY AND CUPS 1943**

Chalk on paper, 33.2 × 49.7 [M1031]
INSCRIPTION 'Wyndham Lewis 1943 Windsor.'
EXHIBITED *'The Talented Intruder'*, Art Gallery of Windsor, Ontario, 1992, no. 61 (and on tour: Glenbow Museum, Calgary; Art Gallery of Ontario, Toronto, 1993)
Private collection

While in Canada, Lewis gained a teaching post at Assumption College in Windsor, Ontario, moving there with his wife Froanna in June 1943 after their long residence in Toronto. This drawing, made shortly after their move, is one of a number of still lifes from 1943–44 showing the paraphernalia of their domestic lives. These tea-service drawings, rather like the intensely personal studies which Lewis made of Froanna, map the contours of their private world. Unlike the more freely inventive of Lewis's wartime works, this scene speaks directly of the isolation and monotony of the Lewises' prolonged stay abroad. JK

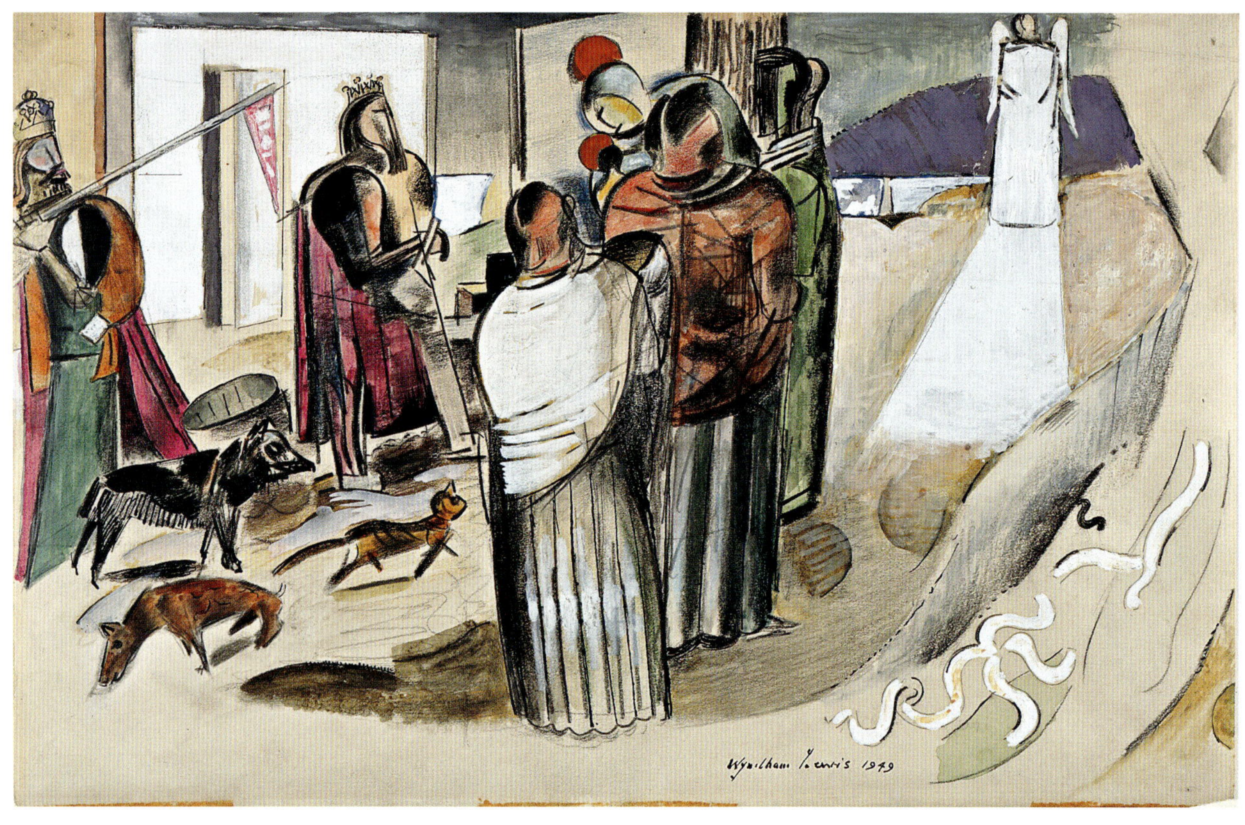


## 52 THE NATIVITY 1949 (started 1941)

Chalk, pen and ink, gouache, watercolour and ink on paper, 29.6 x 45.1 [M1099]
INSCRIPTIONS 'Wyndham Lewis 1949' with an earlier signature and date (1941) erased
EXHIBITED *Word and Image 1 & 2: Wyndham Lewis and Michael Ayrton*, The National Book League, London, 1971, no. 57; *Wyndham Lewis*, The Mayor Gallery, London, 1974, no. 13; *Wyndham Lewis*, Manchester City Art Gallery, Manchester, 1980, no. 154
Wyndham Lewis Memorial Trust: J. Dolman collection

*The Nativity* appears to have been started in 1941 during Lewis's stay in Canada, and only completed some years later, after he had returned to London. The religious subject-matter is typical of a number of Lewis's works of the 1940s, when he produced a series of crucifixions, drawings on the theme of the Creation (see cat. 49) and biblical scenes including the *Adoration* (cat. 46). Here, however, Lewis reworks the traditional iconography of the Nativity into an arcane scene peopled with obscure figures. The Virgin and Child, almost entirely blocked from view by three of the attendant characters, are marked out by red halos, while an angel at the right casts a bright white aura across the scene. The action seems to take place against a coastal shore, outside the Holy Family's primitive dwelling. Lewis's eyesight began to deteriorate in the early 1940s; the strange iconography and occasionally indecipherable passages might be a result of his approaching blindness. JK

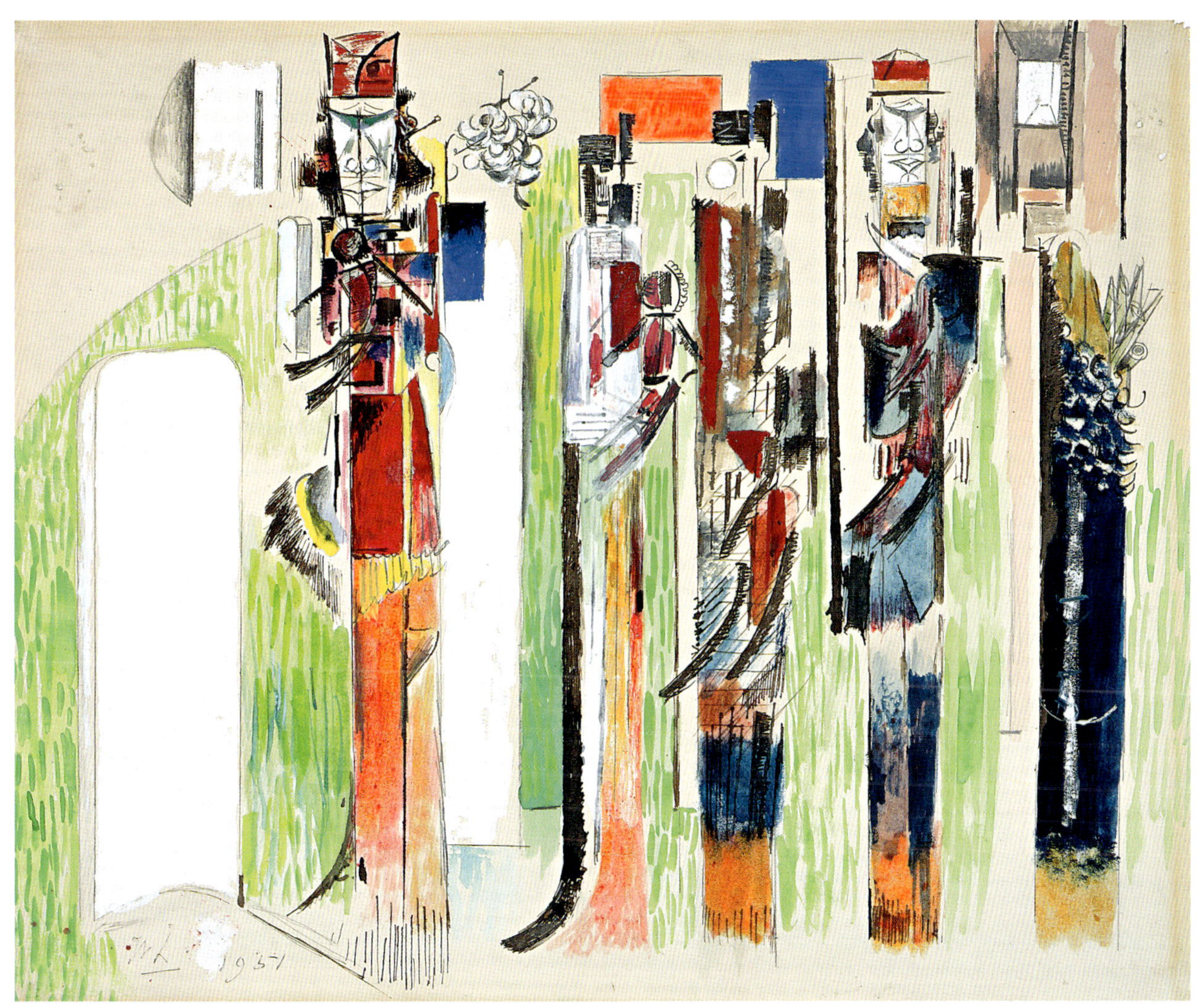

53 **RED FIGURES CARRYING BABIES AND VISITING GRAVES 1951**

Pencil, pen and ink, watercolour and gouache on paper, 33 × 40.3 [M1127]
INSCRIPTIONS 'WL 1951'
EXHIBITED *Seventeen Collectors*, Tate Gallery, London, 1952, no. 263; *Wyndham Lewis and Vorticism*, Tate Gallery, London, 1956, no. 114; *Wyndham Lewis*, Manchester City Art Gallery, Manchester, 1980, no. 154; *Wyndham Lewis: Art and War*, Imperial War Museum, London, 1992
Wyndham Lewis Memorial Trust: J. Bulman collection

This was the last drawing Lewis made before he went blind. In May 1951, writing his final article for *The Listener*, he described how very soon, 'Pushed into an unlighted room, the door banged and locked for ever, I shall … have to light a lamp of aggressive voltage in my mind to keep at bay the night'. Lewis initially identified the figures as French soldiers, but later described them as other-worldly. Fittingly for an artist who had long denounced warfare, this drawing seems to warn against the dangers of conflict, as a new generation is shown the devastation of a war-cemetery. JK

# SELECTED BIBLIOGRAPHY

Date of original publication shown in brackets


PRIMARY TEXTS

Wyndham Lewis, ed., *Blast*, no. 1 (1914) and no. 2 (1915), Black Sparrow Press, Santa Barbara 1981

– *Tarr: The 1918 Version*, ed. Paul O'Keeffe, Black Sparrow Press, Santa Rosa, 1990

– 'Foreword', *Guns*, exhibition catalogue, Goupil Gallery, London, 1919

– 'Foreword', *Group X*, exhibition catalogue, Mansard Gallery, London, 1920

– 'Foreword', *Tyros and Portraits*, exhibition catalogue, Leicester Galleries, London, 1921

– 'Paris versus the World', *The Dial*, vol. 71, no. 1, July 1921, pp. 22–27

– *The Tyro: A review of the arts of painting, sculpture and design*, no. 1 (1921) and no. 2 (1922), Cass, London, 1970

– *The Art of Being Ruled* (1926), ed. Reed Way Dasenbrock, Black Sparrow Press, Santa Rosa, 1989

– *The Lion and the Fox: The Role of the Hero in the Plays of Shakespeare* (1927), Methuen, London, 1966

– *Time and Western Man* (1927), Paul Edwards (ed.), Black Sparrow Press, Santa Rosa, 1993

– *The Enemy: A review of art and literature*, nos. 1 and 2 (1927) and no. 3 (1929), ed. David Peters Corbett, Black Sparrow Press, Santa Rosa, 1994

– 'Preface', *Thirty Personalities*, exhibition catalogue, Lefevre Galleries, London, 1932

– *Blasting and Bombardiering* (1937), Calder & Boyars, London, 1967

– 'Preface', *Paintings and Drawings by Wyndham Lewis*, exhibition catalogue, Leicester Galleries, London, 1937

– *Wyndham Lewis, the Artist: from 'Blast' to Burlington House* (1939), Haskell House, London, 1971

– 'Introduction', *Wyndham Lewis*, exhibition catalogue, Redfern Gallery, London, 1949

– *Rude Assignment: A Narrative of my Career up-to-date*, Hutchinson, London, 1950

– 'The Sea-Mists of the Winter', *The Listener*, 10 May 1951, vol. 45, no. 1158, p. 765

– *Rotting Hill* (1951), ed. Paul Edwards, Black Sparrow Press, Santa Barbara, 1986

– *The Demon of Progress in the Arts* (1954), Methuen, London, 1955

– *Self Condemned*, Methuen, London, 1954

– 'Introduction', *Wyndham Lewis and Vorticism*, exhibition catalogue, Tate Gallery, London, 1956

– *The Letters of Wyndham Lewis*, ed. W.K. Rose, Methuen, London, 1963

– *Wyndham Lewis on Art*, ed. Walter Michel and C.J. Fox, Thames & Hudson, London, 1969

– *The Complete Wild Bodies*, ed. Bernard Lefourcade, Black Sparrow Press, Santa Barbara, 1982 [incorporates *The Wild Body*, 1927]

– *Journey into Barbary: Morocco Writings and Drawings*, ed. C.J. Fox, Black Sparrow Press, Santa Barbara, 1983

– *The Letters of Ezra Pound and Wyndham Lewis*, ed. Timothy Materer, New Directions, New York, 1985

– *Creatures of Habit and Creatures of Change: Essays on art, literature and society, 1914–1956*, ed. Paul Edwards, Black Sparrow Press, Santa Rosa, 1989

SECONDARY TEXTS

David Peters Corbett, ed., *Wyndham Lewis and the Art of Modern War*, Cambridge University Press, Cambridge, 1998

Richard Cork, *Vorticism and its Allies*, exhibition catalogue, Arts Council of Great Britain, London, 1974

– *Wyndham Lewis: The Twenties*, exhibition catalogue, Anthony d'Offay, London, 1984

Paul Edwards, *Wyndham Lewis: Drawings and Watercolours 1910–1920*, Anthony d'Offay, London, 1983

– *Wyndham Lewis: Art and War*, exhibition catalogue, Lund Humphries, London, in association with the Wyndham Lewis Memorial Trust, 1992

– ed., *Volcanic Heaven: Essays on Wyndham Lewis's Painting and Writing*. Black Sparrow Press, Santa Rosa, 1996

– ed., *Blast: Vorticism 1914–1918*, Ashgate, Aldershot, 2000

– *Wyndham Lewis: Painter and Writer*, Yale University Press, New Haven & London, 2000

Dennis Farr, *English Art 1870–1940*, Clarendon Press, Oxford, 1978

Jane Farrington, *Wyndham Lewis*, exhibition catalogue, Lund Humphries, London, in association with City of Manchester Art Galleries, 1980

Toby Avard Foshay, *Wyndham Lewis and the Avant Garde: the Politics of the Intellect*, McGill-Queen's University Press, Montreal, 1992

Charles Handley-Read, *The Art of Wyndham Lewis*, Faber, London, 1951

Charles Harrison, *English Art and Modernism* (1981), Yale University Press, New Haven and London, 1994

Philip Head, *Some Enemy Fight-talk: Aspects of Wyndham Lewis on art and society*, Green Knight Editions, Borough Green, 1999

Richard Humpreys, *Wyndham Lewis*, Tate Publishing, London, 2004

Fredric Jameson, *Fables of Aggression: Wyndham Lewis, the Modernist as Fascist*, University of California Press, Los Angeles and London, 1979

Catherine M. Mastin, Robert Stacey, Thomas Dilworth, *'The Talented Intruder': Wyndham Lewis in Canada, 1939–1945*, exhibition catalogue, The Art Gallery of Windsor, Ontario, 1992

Jeffrey Meyers, *The Enemy: A Biography of Wyndham Lewis*, Routledge & Kegan Paul, London, 1980

Walter Michel, *Wyndham Lewis: Paintings and Drawings*, University of California Press, Berkeley and Los Angeles, 1971

Bradford Morrow and Bernard Lafourcade, *A Bibliography of the Writings of Wyndham Lewis*, Black Sparrow Press, Santa Barbara, 1978

Tom Normand, *Wyndham Lewis the Artist: Holding the Mirror up to Politics*, Cambridge University Press, Cambridge, 1992

Paul O'Keeffe, *Some Sort of Genius: A Life of Wyndham Lewis*, Jonathan Cape, London, 2000

John Rothenstein, *Modern English Painters Volume 2: Lewis to Moore*, Eyre & Spottiswoode, London, 1956

Julian Symons, ed., *The Essential Wyndham Lewis*, Andre Deutsch, London, 1989

Geoffrey Wagner, *Wyndham Lewis: Portrait of the artist as the enemy*, Routledge & Kegan Paul, London, c. 1957

Andrew Wilson, *Wyndham Lewis 1882–1957*, exhibition catalogue, Austin Desmond Fine Art, London, 1990